THE SUBMERGED CONTIN[ENT]
OF
ATLANTIS AND LEMURIA

THEIR HISTORY AND CIVILIZATION

BEING CHAPTERS FROM THE
AKASHIC RECORDS

BY
RUDOLF STEINER
PH. D. (VIENNA)

AUTHORIZED TRANSLATION FROM THE GERMAN
BY
MAX GYSI

AMERICAN EDITION

THE RAJPUT PRESS.

CHICAGO.
1911

ATLANTIS AND LEMURIA

COPYRIGHT 1911, WELLER VAN HOOK, IN THE UNITED STATES OF AMERICA

IN VIEW OF THE MANY UNAUTHORIZED TRANSLATIONS OF DR. RUDOLF STEINER'S WORKS, THE PUBLISHER BEGS TO GIVE NOTICE THAT ALL AUTHORISED EDITIONS, ISSUED UNDER THE EDITORSHIP OF MR. MAX GYSI, BEAR THE SYMBOL OVERLEAF (CROSS IN PENTAGRAM).

MAX GYSI, Editor,
"Adyar," Park Drive,
Hampstead, London, N. W.

CONTENTS

	PAGE
I. FROM THE AKASHIC RECORDS	1
II. OUR ATLANTEAN FOREFATHERS	11
III. TRANSITION OF THE ATLANTEAN INTO THE ARYAN ROOT-RACE	51
IV. THE LEMURIAN ERA	79
V. WOMAN IN THE THIRD ROOT-RACE	99
VI. HUMANITY BEFORE THE DIVISION OF SEX	117
VII. THE BEGINNINGS OF SEX DUALITY (THE ORIGIN OF GOOD AND EVIL)	143
VIII. MAN'S FIRST ANCESTORS	167
IX. THE FIRST, OR POLAR, RACE	195
X. THE SECOND, OR HYPERBOREAN, RACE	213

I

FROM THE AKASHIC RECORDS

It is but a small part of prehistoric human experience which can be learnt by the methods of ordinary history. Historic evidence throws light on only a few thousand years, and even what archaeology, palaeontology and geology can teach us is very limited. Added to this limitation is the untrustworthiness which attaches to everything based upon external evidence. We need only consider how the presentation of some event, even if comparatively recent, or connected with a nation, is totally transformed on the discovery of new historic evidence. We need but compare the descriptions given by different historians of one and the same thing in order to realize at once how insecure is the ground on which we stand. Everything belonging to the outer world of sense is subject to time, and time destroys what in time arises. Now external history depends on what has been preserved to us in time; and no one, dependent only on external evidence, can even say whether that which has been preserved is true.

But everything which arises in time has its origin in the Eternal, and although the Eternal is not accessible to sense-perception, the paths that lead to a perception of the Eternal are available to man. He can so develop the forces that slumber within him as to be able to know this Eternal. In the articles on "How to Attain Knowledge of the Higher Worlds," which have appeared under the title "The Way of Initiation,"* and "Initiation and its Results,"† the method of this training is indicated. In these two books it has been shown that at a certain high stage of knowledge, man can even penetrate to the everlasting sources that underlie the passing things of time. (Let the reader here have patience; these matters can

---

* *"The Way of Initiation,"* by Rudolf Steiner, Ph.D., with a foreword by Annie Besant and some Biographical Notes of the Author by Edouard Schuré. Second edition, price 3/10 inclusive of postage.

† *"Initiation and its Results."* A sequel to the above, price 3/10 post free.

To be obtained from the Theosophical Publishing Society, London, Benares and at the Theosophist office, Adyar.

only be dealt with by degrees.) If a man in the way described has developed his power to know, then, as regards knowledge of the past, he is no longer restricted entirely to outer evidence. Then he can behold that which in the happening is imperceptible to the senses, that which no time can destroy. He presses on from evanescent history to that which does not pass away. It is true that this history is written in other than the ordinary characters, and in the Gnosis, in Theosophy, is called "The Akashic Records." Only a feeble picture of these records can be given in our language, for it is adapted to the uses of the world of sense, and what we name with it receives at once the character of that world. Thus the narrator might give to the uninitiated, to one who cannot yet from his own experience convince himself of the actuality of a distinct spiritual world, the impression of being a mere visionary, if not indeed something worse.

He who has won for himself the power to observe in the spiritual world, there recognizes bygone events in their eternal character. They stand before him, not as dead witnesses of history, but in the fulness of life. In a certain sense, the past events are played out before him. Those who have learnt to read such a living script can look back into a far more distant past than that which external history depicts—and they can also, by direct spiritual perception, describe those matters which history relates, in a far more trustworthy manner than is possible by the latter. In order to avoid a possible error, let it here be at once understood that even mental vision is not infallible. Such perception may also be deceived; it may be inaccurate, crooked, topsy-turvy. Even in this domain nobody, however exalted, is necessarily free from error; therefore no one need take exception if communications that spring from such spiritual sources are not always in full accord. But the trustworthiness of such observations is certainly far greater here than in the outer world of sense, and those communications which, bearing on history and pre-historic times, can be given out by the various Initiates, agree in their essence. In all mystic schools there actually exists such history and pre-history, and such absolute agreement has reigned here for thousands of years that it is impossible to compare it with the agreement existing among ordinary historians even for a century. Initiates describe at all times and in all places essentially the same thing.

After these preliminary remarks, several chapters of the Akashic Records will be repeated here. At the outset those facts will be described which occurred during the existence of the so-called continent of Atlantis, which lay between America and Europe. This part of the surface of our earth was at one time land. Today it is this land which forms the bottom of the Atlantic Ocean. Plato still told of the last remnant of this land—the Island of Poseidonis—lying to the West of

Europe and Africa.

In the little book "The Story of Atlantis" by W. Scott-Elliott,* the reader will learn that the bottom of the Atlantic Ocean was once a continent; that for about 1,000,000 years it was the scene of a civilization, certainly very different from ours of to-day; and that the last remnant of this Continent was submerged nearly 10,000 years B. C. Details completing those given in that book and bearing on this hoary civilization will be given here. While the outward events of the life of these our Atlantean forefathers are more conspicuously the subject of description there, something will here be said of the soul-life, and of the

---

*To be obtained from the Theosophical Publishing Society, London, Benares and at the Theosophist office, Adyar.

inner nature of the conditions under which they lived. The reader must therefore go back in thought to a period lying more than 10,000 years behind us, and to a civilization which had existed for many thousands of years. What is here related, however, took place not only on the continent submerged by the waters of the Atlantic Ocean, but also in the neighbouring regions that now form Asia, Africa, Europe and America—and what subsequently happened in these regions was evolved out of that earlier civilization. As to the sources of the information to be given here, I am for the present obliged to be silent. He who knows anything at all about such sources will understand why this must be so, but circumstances may arise which will make it possible very soon to speak on this subject. How much of the knowledge lying hidden in the womb of the Theosophical movement may gradually be communicated, depends altogether on the attitude of our contemporaries. And now follows the first of the documents which are here to be reproduced.

II

OUR ATLANTEAN FORE-FATHERS

Our Atlantean ancestors differed more from the men of to-day than may be imagined by anyone who is wholly limited to the world of sense for his knowledge. This difference extends not only to the outward appearance, but also to mental capacities. Their science and also their technical arts, their whole civilization, differed much from that of our day. If we go back to the early times of Atlantean humanity we shall find there a mental capacity altogether different from our own.

Logical reasoning, the calculatory combinations upon which all that is produced at the present day is based, were entirely wanting in the early Atlanteans, but in place of these they possessed a highly-developed memory. This memory was one of their most prominent mental faculties. For example, they did not count as we do by the application of certain acquired rules. A multiplication table was something absolutely unknown in early Atlantean times. No one had impressed upon his understanding the fact that three times four were twelve. A person's ability to make such a calculation, when necessary, rested on the fact that he could remember cases of the same or a similar kind. He remembered how this was done on former occasions. Now it must be clearly understood that whenever a new faculty is developed in a being, an old one loses its force and precision. The man of the present day has the advantage over the Atlantean of possessing a logical understanding and an aptitude for combination; but on the other hand his memory power has waned. We now think in ideas, the Atlantean thought in pictures; and when a picture rose in his mind he remembered many other similar pictures which he had formerly seen, and then formed his judgment accordingly. Consequently all education then was quite different from that of later times. It was not intended to provide the child with rules or to sharpen his wits. Rather was life presented to him in comprehensive pictures, so that subsequently he could call to remembrance as much as possible, when dealing with this or that circumstance. When the child had grown up and had reached maturity, he could remember, no matter what he might have to do, that something similar had been shown to him in the days of his instruction. He saw clearly how to act when the new event resembled something already seen. When absolutely new conditions arose, the Atlantean found himself compelled to experiment, while the man of to-day is spared much in this direction, being furnished with a set of rules which he can easily apply in circumstances new to him. Such a system of education gave a strong uniformity to the entire life. Things were done again and again in exactly the same way during very long periods of time. The faithfulness of memory offered no scope for anything at all approaching the rapidity of our own progress. A man did what he had always seen done before; he did not think, he remembered. Not he who had learnt much was held as an authority, but he who had experienced a great deal and could therefore remember much. It would have been imposible in Atlantean times for anyone who had not reached a certain age to be called upon to decide on any affair of importance. Confidence was placed only in one who could look back on a long experience.

What is here said does not refer to Initiates and their schools, for *they* indeed are beyond the average development of their time.

And for admission into such schools, *age* is not the deciding factor, but rather the consideration, whether the candidate in his former incarnations has acquired the ability to assimilate the higher wisdom. The confidence placed in Initiates and their agents in Atlantean times, was not based on the extent of their personal experience, but on the age of their wisdom. For an Initiate, his own personality has ceased to have any importance; he is entirely at the service of the Eternal Wisdom, and therefore the characteristics of any period of time have no weight with him.

Thus, while the power of logical thinking was still wanting, especially in the earlier Atlanteans, they possessed in their highly developed power of memory something which gave a special character to their whole activity. But other powers are always bound up with the nature of one special human force. Memory is nearer to the deeper foundations laid by Nature in man, than is the power of reason, and in connection with the former, other impulses were developed which bore greater resemblance to those lower nature forces than the motive forces of human action at the present day. Thus the Atlantean was master of what is called the Life-Force. Just as we now draw from coal the force of warmth, which is changed into the force of propulsion in our methods of traffic, so did the Atlanteans understand how to use the germinal force of living things in the service of their technical works.

ATLANTIS AND LEMURIA

An illustration of this may be given as follows: Let us think of a grain of corn; in it slumbers a force; this force acts in such a way, that out of the grain of corn the stalk sprouts forth. Nature can awaken this sleeping force in the grain, but the man of to-day cannot do so at will. He must bury the grain in the earth, and leave its awakening to the forces of Nature. The Atlantean could do something more. He knew what to do in order to transform the force in a heap of corn into mechanical power, just as the man of our day can transform into a like power the force of warmth in a heap of coal. In Atlantean times plants were not cultivated merely for use as food; but also in order that the slumbering force in them might be rendered serviceable to their traffic and industry. Just as we have contrivances for transforming the latent force of coal into the power to propel our engines, so had the Atlanteans devices for heating by the use of plant-seeds in which the life-force was changed into a power applicable to technical purposes. In this way were propelled the air-ships of the Atlanteans, which soared a little above the earth. These air-ships sailed at a height rather below that of the mountains of Atlantean times, and they had steering appliances, by means of which they could be raised above these mountains.

We must picture to ourselves that with the advance of time, all the conditions of our earth have greatly changed. These air-ships of the Atlanteans would be quite useless in our days. Their utility lay in the fact that at that time the atmosphere enveloping our earth was much denser than now. Whether, according to the scientific conceptions of the present day, such an increased density of the air can be easily pictured, need not concern us here. Science and logical thought can never, from their very nature, determine what is possible and what impossible. Their task is only to explain what has been proved by experience and observation. And the density of the air here spoken of is, in occult experience, as much a certainty as any given fact of the world of sense can be to-day. And just as firmly established is the fact—perhaps even more inexplicable to the physics and chemistry of our time—that in those days the *water* over the whole earth was much more *fluid* than it is now. And owing to its fluidity, water (being driven by means of the life-force in seeds) could be used by the Atlanteans for technical purposes impossible to-day. On account of the densification of water, it has become impossible to set it in motion and to guide it in the same premeditated manner as was once possible. From this it is sufficiently evident that the civilization of Atlantean times differed fundamentally from our own, and it will also be readily conceivable that the physical nature of an Atlantean was quite different from that of the contemporary man. Water when drunk by the Atlantean could be worked upon by the life-force within his own body in quite another way than is possible in the physical body of to-day. And thus it arose that the Atlantean could use his physical strength at will, quite otherwise than ourselves. He had, as it were, the means within himself of increasing physical forces when he required them for his own use. It is only possible to picture the Atlanteans correctly when one knows that they had conceptions of fatigue and the loss of strength absolutely different from our own.

An Atlantean settlement, as may be gathered from what has already been said, bore a character in no way resembling that of a modern town. But there was a much closer resemblance between it and Nature. We can only give a faint suggestion of the real picture when we say that in early Atlantean times—till about the middle of the third sub-race—a settlement resembled a garden in which the houses formed themselves out of trees whose branches were intertwined in an artistic manner. Whatever the hand of man fashioned at that time grew naturally in like manner. Man, too, felt himself entirely akin to Nature, and so it arose that his social instinct was quite different from our own. Nature is indeed the common property of all men, and whatever the Atlantean built up with Nature for his foundation, he regarded as common property, precisely as the man of to-day thinks it only natural to regard as his own private property that which his acuteness and his reason have produced.

Whoever familiarises himself

with the idea that the Atlanteans were endowed with such mental and physical powers as have been depicted, will likewise learn to understand that at still earlier periods mankind presents an aspect which but very faintly reminds us of what we are accustomed to see to-day. And not only man, but Nature, which surrounds him, has also changed enormously in the course of time.* The forms of plant and animal have altered; the whole of terrestrial Nature has undergone a transformation. Regions of the earth which were formerly inhabited have been de-

---

*With regard to the time-periods at which the conditions shown held sway, some thing more will be said in the course of these communications. For the present the reader is warned not to be surprised if the few figures given him in the previous chapter seem to contradict what he finds elsewhere.

stroyed, and others have arisen.

The forefathers of the Atlanteans lived on a part of the earth which has disappeared, the principal portion of which lay to the south of what is Asia to-day. In Theosophical literature they are called *Lemurians*. After undergoing various stages of evolution the greater number fell into decadence. They became a stunted race whose descendants, the so-called savages, inhabit certain portions of the earth even now. Only a small number of the Lemurians were capable of advancing in their evolution, and it was from these that the Atlantean Race developed. Still later something similar occurred. The great mass of the inhabitants of Atlantis fell into decadence, and the so-called Aryans, to which race belongs the humanity of our present civilization, sprang from a small division of these Atlanteans. According to the nomenclature of the "Secret Doctrine," *Lemurians, Atlanteans,* and *Aryans* are *Root-Races* of humanity. If we think of two such Root-Races preceding the Lemurian, and two following the Aryan in the future, we have altogether *seven.* The one always arises out of the other in the manner pointed out in the case of the Lemurian, Atlantean and Aryan Races. And each Root-Race has physical and mental qualities entirely different from those of that which precedes it. While, for example, the Atlantean brought his memory and everything in connection with it to a high degree of development, the duty of the Aryan of the present is to develop thought-power and all that appertains thereto.

But each Root-Race itself must pass through different stages, and these again are always sevenfold. At the beginning of a time-period belonging to a Root-Race, its leading characteristics appear in an immature state; they gradually reach maturity, and then at last decadence. Thus, the members of a Root-Race are divided into seven sub-races. However, one must not imagine that one sub-race immediately disappeared on the development of a new one. On the contrary, every one of them continued to exist for a long time, while others flourished beside it. Thus there are always dwellers on the earth, living side by side, but showing the most varied stages of evolution.

The first sub-race of the Atlanteans arose from a portion of the Lemurian Race which was greatly advanced and capable of further evolution. For instance, in this latter race the gift of memory showed itself only in its very earliest beginnings, and even so much did not appear until the latest stages of its evolution. It must be realized that a Lemurian could indeed make images of his experiences, but could not preserve them as recollections; he immediately forgot what he had pictured to himself. That, in spite of this, he lived to a certain extent a civilized life,—for instance, that he possessed tools, erected buildings, and so on,—was not due to his own imagination, but to an inner mental force which was instinctive. Yet we must not imagine an instinct similar to that which animals possess at the present time, but an instinct of another order.

The first sub-race of the Atlanteans is called in Theosophical literature the Rmoahal. The memory of this race was especially derived from vivid sense-impressions. Colours which the eye had seen, tones which the ear had heard, continued to operate long within the soul. This was manifested in the fact that the Rmoahals developed *feelings* quite unknown to their Lemurian ancestors. For instance, adherence to that which had been experienced in the past constituted part of such feelings.

Now the development of speech depended on that of memory. As long as man did not remember the past, there could be no narration of experiences by means of speech. And because the first rudiments of memory appeared in the latest Lemurian period, it was only then possible that the ability to give names to things heard and seen could begin to appear. It is only those who have the faculty of recollection who can make any use of a *name* which has been given to an object; and consequently it was in the Atlantean period that speech found its development. And with speech a tie was formed between the human soul and things exterior to man, since he then produced the spoken word from within himself and this spoken word appertained to the objects of the outer world. Through communication by means of speech a new bond also arose between man and man. All this, indeed, was still in an infantile form at the time of the Rmoahals; but nevertheless it distinguished them profoundly from their Lemurian ancestors.

Now the forces in the souls of these first Atlanteans still retained something of the force of Nature. Man was then in a certain manner more nearly related to the Nature-spirits surrounding him than were his descendants. Their soul forces were more Nature forces than are those of the men of the present, and so, too, the spoken word which they uttered had something of the might of Nature. Not only did they name objects, but their words contained a power over things and over their fellow-creatures. The word of the Rmoahal possessed more than mere meaning;

it had also power. When we speak of the magic force of words we indicate something which was a far greater reality at that time, and for those men, than it is for men of the present. When a Rmoahal pronounced a word, this word developed a force akin to that of the object designated by it. Hence it is that words had the power of healing at that time, and that they could hasten the growth of plants, tame the rage of animals, and produce other such effects. All this force gradually faded away among the later Atlantean sub-races. It might be said that that fulness of strength which was a product of Nature wasted away little by little. The men of the Rmoahal race regarded such fulness of strength altogether as a gift from mighty Nature herself; and this relation of theirs with Nature bore for them a religious character. Speech was, to them, something especially sacred, and the misuse of certain tones in which dwelt a significant power was to them an impossibility. Every individual felt that such misuse must bring him terible injury. The magic of such words, they thought, would change into its opposite; that which rightly used would cause a blessing, would bring the author to ruin if wrongly employed. In a certain innocence of feeling the Rmoahals ascribed their power less to themselves than to Divine Nature working in them.

It was otherwise in the second sub-race (the so-called Tlavatli peoples). The men of this race began to feel their own personal value. Ambition, an unknown quality among the Rmoahals, showed itself in them. We might say that the faculty of memory grew into the comprehension of life in communities. He who could look back on certain deeds demanded from his fellow-men some recognition of his ability. He claimed that his work should be held in remembrance, and it was this memory of deeds that was the basis on which rested the election, by a group of men allied to each other, of a certain one as leader. A kind of kingship arose. Indeed, this recognition extended beyond death. The remembrance, the commemoration of forefathers, or of those who, during life, had one merit, arose in this way, and thus in single family groups there grew up a kind of religious reverence for the dead—in other words, ancestor worship. This has continued to spread into much later times and has taken the most varied forms. Among the Rmoahals a man was still esteemed only according to the degree in which for the moment he was able to make himself valuable by the greatness of his power. Did anyone want recognition for what he had done in former days, then he must show by new deeds that he still possessed the old power. He must call to remembrance his old achievements by the performance of new ones. That which had once been done was valueless in itself. Not until the second sub-race was the personal character of a man of so much account that his past life was taken into consideration in the estimation of it.

A further result of the power of thought in drawing men to live together appeared in the fact that groups of men were formed who were united by the remembrance of deeds done in company. The forming of such groups originally depended wholly upon the forces of Nature, on their common parentage. By his own intelligence man had as yet added nothing to that which Nature had made of him. One mighty personality now enlisted a great company to share in a common undertaking, and the remembrance of this work, being retained by all, built up a social group.

This manner of living together in social groups only impressed itself forcibly when the third sub-race (the Toltec) was reached. It was therefore the men of this race who first founded what may be called a commonwealth, the earliest kind of statecraft. The leadership, the government, of this commonwealth passed from ancestors to descendants. That which had formerly continued only in the memory of their fellow-men the father now transferred to the son. The deeds of their forefathers would be kept in remembrance by the whole race. The achievements of an ancestor continued to be cherished by his descendants. However, we must clearly understand that in those times men really had the power to transfer their gifts to their offspring. Education was based upon the representation of life in comprehensive pictures. And the efficacy of this education depended on the personal force which proceeded from the teacher. It was not an intellectual power which he sought to excite, but rather those gifts which were more instinctive in character. By such a system of education the father's ability was really in most cases transferred to the son.

Under conditions like these, *personal experience* won for itself more and more importance in the third sub-race. When one group of human beings severed itself from another group, it brought with it for the foundation of its new community the vivid recollection of what it had experienced in its former surroundings. But all the same these memories contained something with which they were not in sympathy, something in which they did not feel at ease. In this connection, therefore, they sought something new, and thus conditions improved with every new settlement of the kind. And it was only natural that the improved conditions should find imitators. These were the facts on which rested the foundation of those flourishing commonwealths that arose in the time of the third sub-race, and are described in Theosophical literature. The personal experiences undergone found support from those who were *initiated* into the eternal laws of mental development. Mighty rulers received initiation in order that personal ability might have its full provision. A man gradually prepares himself for initiation by his personal ability. He must first develop his forces from below upwards, so that enlightenment may then be imparted to him from above. Thus arose the King-Initiates and Leaders of the people among the Atlanteans. In their hands lay a tremendous amount of power, and great, too, was the reverence paid to them.

But in this fact lay also the cause of their fall. The development of memory led to enormous personal power. The individual began to wish for influence by means of this power of his; and the greater the power grew, the more did he desire to use it for himself. The ambition which he had developed became selfishness, and this gave rise to a misuse of the forces. When we consider what the Atlanteans were able to do by their command of the life-force, we can then understand that such misuse must have had tremendous consequences. An enormous power over Nature could be placed at the service of personal self-love.

And this was what happened in full measure during the period of the fourth sub-race (the original Turanians). The members belonging to this race, who were instructed in the mastery of the forces mentioned, made manifold use of these to satisfy their wayward wishes and desires. But these forces put to such a use naturally destroy one another in their action. It is as if the feet of a man wilfully moved forwards while at the same time the upper part of his body desired to go backwards.

Such destructive action could only be arrested by the cultivation of a higher force in man. This was thought-power. The effect of logical thinking is to restrain selfish personal wishes. We must seek the origin of this logical thought in the fifth sub-race (the original Semites). Men began to go beyond the simple remembrance of the past, they began to *compare* their various experiences. The faculty of judgment developed, and wishes and desires were regulated according to this discernment. Man began to calculate, to combine. He learnt to work in thoughts. Whereas formerly he had abandoned himself to every wish, he now asked himself whether, on reflection, he approved of the wish. While the men of the fourth sub-race wildly rushed after the satisfaction of their desires, those of the fifth began to hearken to the inner voice. And this inner voice had the effect of checking the desires, even if it could not crush the demands of the selfish personality.

Thus did the fifth sub-race implant within the human soul, the interior impulses of action. In his own soul man must decide what to do and what to leave undone. But, while man thus gained thought-power inwardly, his command over the external forces of Nature was being lost. The forces of the mineral kingdom can be controlled only by means of this combining thought, not by the life-power. It was therefore at the cost of the mastery of the life-force that the fifth sub-race developed thought-power. But it was just by so doing that they created the germs of a further evolution of humanity. Now it is no longer possible for thought alone,—working entirely within the man, and no longer able to command Nature directly,—to bring about such devastating results as did the misused forces of earlier times, even if the personality, self-love, and selfishness were ever so great. Out of this fifth sub-race was chosen its most gifted portion, which outlived the destruction of the Fourth Race and formed the nucleus of the Fifth,—the Aryan Race, whose task it is to bring to perfection the power of thought and all that belongs thereto.

The men of the sixth sub-race —the Akkadian—trained their thought-power still more highly than did the fifth. They distinguished themselves from the so-called ancient Semites by bringing into use in a wider sense the faculty mentioned. It has been said that the development of thought-power did not indeed allow the demands of the selfish personality to attain such destructive results as were possible in earlier races—but that, nevertheless, these demands were not killed out by it. The original Semites at first regulated their personal affairs as their reason suggested. In place of crude desires and lust, prudence appeared. Other conditions of life presented themselves. Whereas the races of former times inclined to recognize as their leader him whose deeds were deeply engraved in the memory, or who could look back on a life rich in recollections, such a *role* was now rather adjudged to the wise man, and if formerly that was considered decisive which was still fresh in the memory, so now that was regarded as best which appealed most strongly to the reason. Under the influence of thought, men once clung to a thing till it was considered insufficient, and then in the latter case it came about naturally that he who had a novelty capable of supplying a want should find a hearing. A love of novelty and a longing for change were, however, developed by this thought-power. Everyone wanted to carry out what his own sagacity suggested, and thus it is that restlessness begins to appear in the fifth sub-race, leading in the sixth to the necessity of placing under general laws the capricious ideas of the single individual. The glory of the states of the third sub-race lay in the order and harmony caused by a common memory. In the sixth, this order had to be obtained by deliberately constructed laws. Thus in the sixth sub-race must be sought the origin of law and legislation. And during the third sub-race the segregation of a group of human beings took place only when in a manner they were compelled to leave because they no longer felt comfortable within the prevailing conditions brought about by recollection. It was essentially different in the sixth. The calculating power of thought sought novelty, as such; it urged men to enterprise and new undertakings. Thus the Akkadians were an enterprising people inclined towards colonization. It was commerce especially that fed the young and germinating power of thought and judgment.

In the seventh sub-race—the Mongolian—thought-power also developed, but in them existed qualities of the earlier sub-races, especially of the fourth, in a much greater degree than in the fifth and sixth. They remained true to their sense of memory. And so they came to the conclusion that the most ancient must also be the wisest, must be that which could best defend itself against the attack of thought. They had indeed lost the command of the life-force, but that which developed in them as thought-power had in itself something of the power of this life-force. It is true they had lost the power over life, but never the direct, instinctive belief in the existence of such a power. This force, indeed, became to them their God in Whose service they performed everything which they considered right. Thus they appeared to their neighbours to be possessed of a mystic power, and the latter yielded to it in blind faith. Their posterity in Asia and in some European regions showed, and still show, much of this peculiarity.

The power of thought implanted in man could only attain its full value in evolution when, in the Fifth Race, it acquired a new impulse. After all, the Fourth could only place this power at the service of that which had been fostered by the gift of memory. It was not until the Fifth was reached that such forms of life were attained as could find their instrument in the faculty of thought.

III

TRANSITION OF THE ATLANTEAN INTO THE ARYAN ROOT-RACE

The following communications refer to the transition of the fourth (Atlantean) Root-Race into the fifth (Aryan), to which belongs the civilized mankind of the present day. He only will estimate them correctly who is able to grasp the idea of evolution in its fullest meaning. Everything that comes to the notice of man in his surroundings is in a condition of development. And it must also be remembered that the peculiar characteristic of men of our fifth

Root-Race, consisting in the use of *thought*, has but just been developed. Indeed, it is this Root-Race that slowly and gradually brings the power of thought to maturity. The man of the present makes up his mind and carries out his decision on the strength of his own thought. With the Atlanteans this capacity was only in preparation. Not their *own* thoughts, but those which flowed in upon them from Beings of a higher kind, influenced their will, which was thus guided, in a sense, from without. He who makes himself familiar with this conception of evolution in regard to man, and who learns to admit that he was, in pre-historic times and as an inhabitant of the earth, of an altogether different constitution will also be able to advance to the conception of those wholly different Beings to whom reference is made in these communications. The development which is under consideration occupied enormous periods of time. Details of this will be shown more circumstantially in the following communications.

What has previously been said about the fourth Root-Race, the Atlantean, refers to the great general mass of mankind. But the latter found themselves under leaders who towered high above them in ability. The wisdom possessed by these leaders, and the powers of which they were masters, could not be obtained through any earthly education, but were imparted to them by entities of a high rank, and not pertaining directly to the earth. It was, therefore, quite natural that the great mass of mankind regarded these, their leaders, as Beings of a higher kind, as "messengers" of the gods. For that which these leaders knew and were able to achieve could not have been accomplished by means of human sense-organs or human understanding. They were worshipped as "Divine Messengers," and their precepts, commands, and instructions were accepted. By such Beings mankind was instructed in sciences, arts and the construction of tools. And such "Divine Messengers" either directed the communities themselves, or instructed such men as were sufficiently developed in the arts of governing. These leaders were said "to hold intercourse with gods" and to be initiated by these themselves in the laws according to which mankind was to develop. And this was in accordance with fact. This initiation, this intercourse with the gods, occurred at places quite unknown to the populace. "Temples of Mysteries" was the name given to these places of initiation, and it was from their midst that mankind was governed.

That which took place in the Temples of Mysteries was, accordingly, incomprehensible to the populace, and only very slightly did these understand the purposes of their great leaders. The people could, indeed, understand with their senses only what happened immediately on the earth, not what was revealed from higher worlds. Consequently the teachings of the leaders had also to be clad in a form which was unlike the form used in the communication of earthly matters. The language used in the mysteries between the gods and their messengers was, indeed, no earthly tongue, nor were the forms assumed by the gods in their manifestations of an earthly kind. "In fiery clouds" did they, the higher spirits, appear to their messengers, in order to instruct them how men were to be guided. Only a man can appear in human form; entities whose faculties surpass the human level must manifest under forms which are not to be found among those of earth.

The fact that the "Messengers of the Gods" could receive the revelations was owing to their attainment of the highest degree of development among their human brothers. They had already, in earlier stages of evolution, gone through what the majority of men have yet to experience. Only in a special way did they belong to this contemporaneous mankind. They could assume the human form, but their psycho-spiritual faculties were superhuman in character. They were, therefore, divine-human, double entities. Hence they might also be described as higher spirits who had assumed human bodies, in order to help mankind further along its earthly path. Their true home was not on the earth. These entities guided man without being able to communicate to him the principles according to which they were leading him. For up to the fifth subrace of the Atlanteans, the original Semites, men had absolutely no capacity whatever wherewith to grasp these principles. Not till the power of thought began to develop in this sub-race did such capacity exist. But this faculty developed slowly and gradually. Even the last sub-races of the Atlanteans could as yet understand very little of the principles of their divine leaders. They began by having a very vague presentiment of such principles. Consequently, their conceptions and also the laws mentioned in connection with their civic institutions, were intuitive rather than definitely thought out.

The chief leader of the fifth Atlantean sub-race had for his object to bring it gradually to such a point that it could, later on, and after the disappearance of the Atlantean mode of living, initiate a new one, such as would be completely regulated by the power of thought.

Now we must realize that the end of the Atlantean era is characterized by these groups of human entities. There are: firstly, the so-called "Messengers of the Gods," who were advanced far beyond the great mass of people, teaching Divine Wisdom and performing divine deeds. Secondly, there was the great mass itself, in which the power of thought was in a state of torpor, although it possessed other natural faculties which have since been lost. Thirdly, there was a smaller number of such as developed the thinking capacity. These, it is true, gradually lost the primeval faculties of the Atlanteans; but they developed instead the capacity to grasp in thought the principles of the "Messengers of the Gods." The second group of human entities was destined to die out gradually. The third, however, admitted of such an education by the entities of the first group that it could henceforward take over its own guidance.

From the midst of this third group, selection was made by the aforesaid chief leader (who is known in Theosophical literature, by the name of the Manu) of those most capable of forming the nucleus of a new mankind. These fittest people were to be found in the fifth sub-race. The thought power of the sixth and seventh sub-races was in a certain way already on the downward path, and no longer fit for further development. The best qualities of the best men were to be developed. This was achieved by the leader sequestering the elect in a particular spot of the earth—in Central Asia—and freeing them from every influence of those left behind or gone astray. The task undertaken by the leader was to conduct his disciples so far on that they could grasp in their own souls and through their own thought the principles according to which they were previously directed and which they faintly understood. Men were now meant to understand the divine powers which they had formerly followed blindly. So far, the gods had led men through their messengers; henceforth men should *know* of these divine Beings. They were to consider themselves as the executive organs of divine Providence.

This isolated group had to face an important change. The divine leader was in their midst in human form. From such divine messengers mankind had previously received directions or commands, as to what was to be done or left undone. It had been taught in sciences which referred to what could be observed by the senses. Men suspected the fact of a divine government of the world, they felt as much in their own actions; but a clear knowledge of this fact they had not. Their leader now spoke to them quite differently. He taught them that invisible powers governed what was visibly before them; and that they themselves were servants of these invisible powers; that, with their thoughts they had to execute the laws of these powers; and that the invisible spiritual element was the Creator and Preserver of the visible material world. Hitherto they had looked up to their visible messengers of the gods, to those superhuman Initiates of whom he who talked to them thus was himself one, and by whom they were directed as to what to do or to avoid. Now, however, they were found worthy of being instructed by the divine messenger of the gods. Powerful was the injunction impressed again and again on his followers: "Hitherto ye have seen those who were your Leaders, but there are higher Leaders whom ye see not, and ye are subject to these Leaders. Fulfil the commands of the God whom ye see not, and obey Him of whom ye can make to yourself no image." Thus sounded, from the lips of the great Leader, the new and highest commandment, prescribing the worship of a God whom no image visible to the senses could resemble, of whom, therefore, none such should be made. An echo of this great primary commandment of the fifth race is heard in the well-known phrase: "Thou shalt have none other gods before me. Thou shalt not make unto thee any graven image, nor the *likeness* of any form that is in heaven above, or that is in the earth beneath, or that is in the water under the earth." (Exodus xx, 3-4.)

Assisting the chief leader (Manu), there were other messengers of the gods who executed his designs with regard to particular branches of life, and helped in the development of the new race. For the object was to arrange the whole of life conformably with the new conception of a divine government of the world. The thoughts of men were to be turned in every respect from the visible to the invisible. Life is determined by natural forces. The course of this human life depends on day and night, winter and summer, sunshine and rain. How these momentous visible facts are connected with the invisible (divine) forces, and how man should act so as to live in accordance with these invisible powers, all this was shown to him. All knowledge and all work were to be pursued in this sense. In the course of the stars and in atmospheric conditions, man was to see the decrees of Providence, the expression of divine Wisdom. Astronomy and Meteorology were taught in this sense. And man was to bring his work, his moral life, into harmony with the laws of the divine, that are so rich in wisdom. Life was ordered according to divine commandments, since in the course of the stars, in meteorological conditions, etc., divine thoughts were fathomed. Man was to bring his works into harmony with dispositions of the gods through sacrificial deeds.

It was the intention of the Manu to direct everything in human life towards the higher worlds. All human action, all arrangements were to bear a religious character. In this way, the Manu wished to lead the way to that which constitutes the special task of the fifth Root-Race. This Race was to learn to guide itself onward through its own thoughts. Such self-determination, however, can lead to salvation only when man gives his own self also to the service of the higher powers. Man should make use of his thinking capacity; but this power of thought should be uplifted by mindfulness of the Divine.

To grasp completely what happened at that time, it is also necessary to know that the development of the thinking capacity, beginning with the fifth sub-race of the Atlanteans, brought about a still further consequence. In a certain direction men acquired branches of knowledge and performed acts which were in no immediate connection with what the Manu had to consider as his proper task. These acquirements and arts lacked, first of all, the religious character. They dawned on man at a time when his only thought was to exploit them for his own advantage, for his personal wants. To such acquirements belongs, for instance, that of Fire in its application to human industry. At the beginning of the Atlantean era man had no need of fire, as the vital force was still at his disposal. With the decrease of his ability to avail himself of this force, he was obliged to learn how to fashion his tools and implements from so-called lifeless things. Here the use of fire became most advantageous. And it was likewise with regard to other natural forces. Man had also learned to make use of these forces without being conscious of their divine origin. This, indeed, was inevitable. Man was not to be *forced* to link these things, which assisted his own mentality, with the divine order of things. This he was rather meant to do voluntarily in his thoughts. The intention of the Manu was, then, to evoke in men a spontaneous need to establish a connection between such things and the higher order of the world. Men could, as it were, choose whether they would exploit the acquired knowledge for purely personal benefit, or use it in the religious service of a higher world. Just as man had previously been forced to consider himself as a part of the divine ruling of the world, from which there flowed in on him, for instance, the mastery of the vital force without any need of mental effort, so now he could also make use of natural forces without giving thought to the divine. Of those whom the Manu had gathered round himself, all were not ripe for the change. Indeed very few of them were so. And only from these could the nucleus of the new race be actually formed by the Manu. It was, then, only with this small number that the Manu retired, in order to further their development, while the rest became merged in the general mass of mankind. It was then from this small number of men, thus finally grouped round the Manu, that were derived all the true germs of the progress of the fifth Root-Race up to the present time. Thus, however, it becomes plain that the whole development of this fifth Root-Race displays two characteristic features. One of these distinguishes those who are animated by higher ideals, and who consider themselves as children of a divine universal power; the other appears in those who make every-

ATLANTEAN INTO ARYAN

thing subservient only to personal interests, to selfish ends.

This little band remained with the Manu until it had become strong enough to act in the new spirit, and until its members could set forth to impart this new spirit to that portion of mankind which remained over from the preceding races. This new spirit naturally assumed a different character with various nations, according to the different phases of their development. The old surviving characteristics became mixed with what the messengers of the Manu brought into the various parts of the world, and in this way manifold new cultures and civilizations arose.

The fittest personalities of those surrounding the Manu were chosen to become initiated little by little into his divine wisdom, so that they might become teachers to the rest. Thus it was that along with the old messengers of the gods there now arose a new kind of Initiates. These were they who developed their mentality in exactly the same manner as the rest of their fellow-men. The divine messengers of old—and the Manu—had not done so. Their development belongs to higher worlds. They brought their higher wisdom into earthly relations. What they gave to mankind was "a gift from on high." Before the middle of the Atlantean era men were not advanced far enough to grasp with their own faculties the import of divine decrees. Now—in the period indicated—they were to reach this stage. Their earthly thought was to rise to the conception of the divine. Human Initiates united

ATLANTEAN INTO ARYAN

themselves with those who were superhuman. This signifies an important change in the development of humanity. The first Atlanteans had not yet the choice of viewing their leaders as divine messengers or of not doing so. For what these accomplished appeared, perforce, as a deed of the higher worlds. A divine origin was stamped on it. On account of their power, the divine messengers of the Atlantean era were therefore sanctified Beings, surrounded by the lustre conferred on them by this power. The human Initiates of the subsequent era, if considered externally, are men among men. To be sure, they remained in touch with the higher worlds, receptive of the revelations and appearances of the messengers of the gods. Only on exceptional occasions, in the case of a higher necessity, they made use of certain powers, conferred on them from that source. Then did they perform feats which men failed to interpret in terms of the known laws, and therefore rightly viewed as miracles. Nevertheless it is the higher purpose of all this to place men on their own feet, to develop perfectly their mentality. The human Initiates are now the mediators between the people and the higher powers; and Initiation alone qualifies one for intercourse with the messengers of the gods.

The human Initiates, the holy teachers, became, then, in the beginning of the fifth Root-Race the leaders of the rest of mankind. The great priest-kings of pre-historic times—attested to, if not historically, at least mythologically—

belong to this class of Initiates. The higher messengers of the gods gradually withdrew from this earth, handing over the leadership to these human Initiates, but still assisting them by deed and word. Were this not so man would not attain to a free use of his mentality. The world stands under divine guidance; but man should not be forced to acknowledge this fact, but should do so in consequence of the free exercise of his mental capacity. Only when he has attained to this do the Initiates gradually unveil to him their secrets. But this cannot be attained suddenly. Rather is the whole development of the fifth Root-Race a slow path to this goal. At first the Manu himself still led his flock like children, but afterwards the leadership was gradually transferred to human Initiates. And, to-day, the progress still continues to consist in a mixture of conscious and unconscious acting and thinking on the part of men. Only at the end of the fifth Root-Race, when, after the progress made in the course of the sixth and seventh sub-races, a sufficiently large number of men will be ready to receive knowledge, the greatest Initiate will be able to reveal himself to them publicly. And *this* human Initiate will then be able to take over the further general leadership, just as the Manu had done at the end of the fourth Root-Race. The education of the fifth Root-Race has therefore as its aim the production of a larger portion of mankind who shall attain so far as to follow freely a human Manu, just as was done by the nucleus of this fifth race with regard to the divine Manu.

———

IV

THE LEMURIAN ERA

The following contains a fragment from the Akashic records which refers to a very remote prehistoric epoch in the development of mankind. This epoch precedes that which has been delineated in the previous chapters. The subject is the third human Root-Race, which, in Theosophical books, is said to have dwelt on the Lemurian continent. This continent lay—according to these books—in the south of Asia, but extended roughly from Ceylon to Madagascar. Also the modern southern Asia and parts of Africa belonged to it. Although in the reading of the Akashic records all possible precaution has been observed, it must nevertheless be emphasized that in no case must a dogmatic character be claimed for these communications. Merely to read of things and happenings so far removed from the present is by no means easy, but a translation of what has been seen and deciphered into the language of our time entails almost insuperable obstacles. Dates will be given later. They will be better grasped when we have given an account of the whole Lemurian era, and also of that which embraces the fifth Root-Race up to the present time. The things which are here communicated are surprising even to the occultist when he reads them for the first time—although the word "surprise" does not quite suit the case. This, however, is why he is allowed to communicate them only after a most careful examination.

* * *

The fourth (Atlantean) Root-Race was preceded by the so-called *Lemurian*. In the course of its development the earth and mankind underwent transformations of the greatest significance. Nevertheless, something will first be said about the character of this Root-Race subsequently to these transformations, a delineation of which will follow. This Root-Race as a whole had not yet developed memory. Men were able, it is true, to form conceptions of things and events; but these conceptions did not remain in the memory, and in consequence men did not possess language in its true sense. What they could produce in this connection were rather natural sounds which expressed their sensations of pleasure, joy, pain, and so on, but which did not designate external things. Their mental conceptions, however, had quite another power than those of later men. They influenced their surroundings by means of this power. Other men, animals, plants and even inanimate objects could feel this action and were worked upon by mere mind-images. Thus the Lemurian could communicate with his fellow-men without the need of speech. This intercourse consisted of a kind of "thought-reading." The power of his conceptions was derived by the Lemurian immediately from the things that surrounded him. It flowed on him from the power of growth in plants, from the vital energy in animals. Thus did he understand plants and animals in their inner working and life. Indeed, he thus understood even the physical and chemical forces of inanimate things. In building anything, he did not need first to calculate the bearing-capacity of a trunk or the weight of a block of stone: he could *see* how much the trunk could bear, how the block would settle through its weight. The Lemurian built in this way without any art of engineering, but with the certainty of a kind of instinct working out as imagination. And withal he had his body under great control. If necessary he could steel his arm through a mere effort of will. Consequently he could, for instance, raise enormous burdens. Just as the Atlantean disposed of the vital energy, so the Lemurian was master of his will. He was—let not the expression be misunderstood—a born magician in all spheres of the lower human activities.

The main object, too, of the Lemurians was to develop the will, and the power of conception. This was the ruling motive in the education of children. Boys were hardened in the most energetic manner. They had to learn to face dangers, to overcome pain, to perform daring deeds. Those who could not bear tortures or face dangers were not considered useful members of society, but were allowed to perish in the course of their hardships. What the Akashic records show in regard to this method of rearing children surpasses all that the present man can picture to himself in his wildest fancy. The endurance of heat up to scorching point or the piercing of the body with sharp points were quite common occurrences. The training of girls was different. It is true that hardening was also their lot, but the chief aim lay here in the development of a powerful imagination. For instance, girls were exposed to a storm that they might feel its terrible beauty with calmness; they had to witness fights between men, fearlessly, feeling only admiration for the display of strength and prowess. A disposition to dreaming, to revelling in fancy, was in this way fostered in girls; but this disposition was exceptionally prized, and in the absence of memory there was no chance of its degeneration. These dreamy or imaginative conceptions lasted only while there was an external occasion for them. So far, then, they were well equipped for external things. They did not lose themselves in the fathomless. It was the imaginative and visionary in Nature herself that sank down into the soul of woman.

Until the end of their era the Lemurians had no dwellings in our sense of the word. They lived in natural shelters: for instance, in caves which they modified according to their needs. At a later period they built such caves in the earth; and then they developed great skill in such building. But it must not be thought that they did not also erect artificial build-

THE LEMURIAN ERA.

ings, although these did not serve as dwellings. They originated in the earlier period from the need of giving to the things of nature a form moulded by man. Hills were re-moulded so that man might find pleasure and gratification in their form. For the same reason stones were joined together, and this was done also with the aim of making them serve some useful purpose. The places where children were hardened were surrounded by walls of this kind. But ever grander and more ingenious, toward the end of this epoch, became the structures devoted to the worship of "divine Wisdom and divine Art." These edifices were in every respect different from what served, at a later stage, as temples, for they were also places of instruction and scientific study. Whoever was found fit was permitted to become initiated into the science of universal laws and the application of these laws. Whereas the Lemurian was a born magician, this talent for art and insight was here cultivated. Only those could be admitted who, through every process of hardening, had become invincible in the highest degree. That which transpired in these institutions remained the most profound secret to all but the few. Here the knowledge and mastery of natural forces was learnt by immediate perception. But this cognizance was a kind of transformation of the natural forces into the power of will in man. Thereby he could himself achieve what Nature achieves. What mankind accomplished later by means of reflection or combination was then a kind of instinctive activity. Of course, in this connection the word "instinct" must not be used in the sense in which it is usually applied to the animal world, for the achievements of the Lemurians rank immeasurably higher than all that the animal world can produce instinctively. They far surpassed all that mankind through memory, intellect and imagination has since acquired in arts and sciences. To make this more clearly understood one might call these teaching-places "high-schools of the powers of will and of the clairvoyant power of forming conceptions." From them proceeded such men as became in every respect rulers of the others. It is difficult to-day to give in words a correct conception of all these conditions, for everything on earth has since undergone a change. Nature herself and all human life were different then; and consequently human labour and the relation of man to man were quite other than what is customary now.

The atmosphere was as yet much denser than later during the Atlantean era; and water was much more fluid. Also that which now forms our firm earth-crust was not yet hardened to the same extent as later. The vegetable and animal worlds were advanced only to the stage of amphibious animals, of birds and the lower mammals, and of growths analagous to our palms and similar trees. But all forms were different from those of the present. What is now found small in size was then de-

THE LEMURIAN ERA

veloped to gigantic proportions. Our small ferns were then trees which formed mighty forests. The higher mammals of to-day were not in existence at that time. On the other hand a great portion of mankind was at so low a stage of development that it must be described as altogether animal. In fact, the foregoing description of men applies only to a small number. The remainder lived on the animal level. Indeed, these animal-men were, in their external form, and in their mode of living, altogether different from that small number. They hardly differed from the lower mammals, whom in a way they also resembled in form.

A few words must also be added as to the significance of the places of worship previously mentioned.

It was not exactly religion that was fostered there. It was "divine Wisdom and Art." Man felt what was given him there to be a direct gift from the spiritual world-powers, and when he shared in this gift he looked upon himself as a "servant" of these universal powers. He felt himself "consecrated" in opposition to all that was unholy. If one would speak of religion at this stage of mankind, one might call it "religion of the will." Religious feeling and consecration lay in this, that a man guarded the powers conferred on him as a "secret" deep and divine, and that he led such a life as sanctified his power. Very great were the awe and reverence with which persons possessed of such powers were regarded by others; nor was this enjoined by laws or in any other way, but was the result of the direct power exercised by such men. One who was not initiated found himself quite naturally under the magical influence of the Initiates, and as a matter of course the latter considered themselves consecrated persons. For in their temples they were in a true sense partakers in the working of natural forces. They gazed into the creative laboratory of Nature. What they experienced was intercourse with the Beings who work at the building of the world itself. This may be called an intercourse with the gods, and what developed later as "Initiation" or "Mysteries" sprang from this original mode of intercourse between men and the gods. In later times this intercourse was bound to undergo a transformation, because the human conception, the human spirit, assumed other forms.

Special importance attaches to one point connected with the progress of the Lemurian development in consequence of the mode of life which was pursued by the women. They developed, by this way of living, special human powers. The unity of their imaginative power with Nature became the basis of a higher development of the imaginative life. Through their senses they drew into themselves the forces of Nature, and allowed these to react on their souls. Thus were the germs of memory formed. And with memory there entered into the world the capacity to form the first and very simplest of moral conceptions. The culture of the will in the masculine element brought, at the outset, no development of the mind. Man followed instinctively either natural impulses or influences emanating from the Initiates. Womankind gave birth to the first conceptions of "good and evil." Here they began on the one hand to love that which made a special impression on their imaginative life, and on the other hand to hate its opposite. While the rule exercised by the masculine element was directed more to the external effect of the powers of will, to the management of natural powers,—in the feminine element there arose at the same time an impulse through the feelings, through the inner personal human powers. He only can comprehend the development of mankind correctly who realizes that the first steps in advance in the sphere of imagination were made by women. The development of habits dependent on the meditative, imaginative life, on the cultivation of memory which formed the nucleus of a life of order, of a sort of moral life, came from this side. Whereas man perceived and exercised natural forces, women became the first *interpreter* of these. It was a new and special mode of life that here arose—that of Thought. This mode had something far more personal than that of men. Now we must understand that this mode of women was really itself a kind of clairvoyance, even although it differed from the magic of the will on the part of man. Woman was, in her soul, receptive to another kind of spiritual power,—to such as appealed more to the element of feeling, and less to the spiritual element to which man was subjected. There emanated thus from men an influence which was more naturally divine, from women one that was more psychically divine.

V

WOMAN IN THE THIRD ROOT-RACE

The development undergone by woman during the Lemurian era qualified her for an important *role* on the earth in connection with the beginning of the next Atlantean Root-Race. This was ushered in under the influence of highly developed entities who were acquainted with the laws of the moulding of races, and who were capable of turning the existing forces of human nature into such courses as led to the formation of a new race. Later on a special reference will be made to these entities. For the present suffice it to say that superhuman wisdom and power were immanent in them. They separated a small number of Lemurian men and appointed them to become the progenitors of the subsequent Atlantean Race. The place chosen lay in the torrid zone. The men of this little clan attained, under their guidance, the mastery of Nature's forces. They were full of energy and knew how to wrest from Nature treasures of many kinds. They knew how to cultivate fields and how to utilize their fruits. Through the training to which they had been subjected (compare previous chapter) they had become men of strong will. It was in woman, however, that the mind and soul were developed, for it was in her that memory and imagination, and all connected therewith, were found to have been already fostered.

The leaders to whom reference has been made brought about an arrangement of the little flock into small groups, and they entrusted women with the ordering and arranging of these groups. Women had acquired by means of their memory the faculty of utilizing for the future all the experiences that they had once known. That which had proved valuable yesterday was turned by them to present advantage; and they were clearly aware that it would likewise be useful to-morrow. The arrangements of the communal life came thus from women. Under their influence the notions of "good and evil" were developed. Through their reflective life they had acquired an understanding of Nature. Out of their observations of Nature grew the ideas according to which they guided the actions of men. The leaders arranged things in such wise that the will-power and super-abundant energy of men were ennobled and purified by the "soul" in woman. Of course, all this is to be considered as at an elementary stage. The words of our languages are too apt to suggest ideas derived from contemporary life.

Indirectly, through the awakened psychical life of women did the leaders develop that of the men. In the above-mentioned colony, the influence of women was therefore very great. They were consulted whenever it was desired to interpret the signs of

WOMAN IN THE THIRD ROOT-RACE

Nature. The whole mode of their psychic life was, however, still such that it was ruled by the "secret" psychic powers of women. To give an approximate, if not quite adequate, conception of this state, one might speak of a somnambulistic perception on the part of these women. The secrets of Nature were revealed to them and the impulses of their actions were imparted in a kind of higher dream-state. Everything to them was the expression of spiritual powers and appeared in the form of psychic faculties and visions. They abandoned themselves to the mystic working of their psychic powers. They were prompted to their actions by "inner voices" or by that which was told them by plants, animals, and stones, the wind and the clouds, or the rustling of the trees.

From soul conditions of such a kind arose that which may be called human religion. The psychic element in Nature and in human life came gradually to be reverenced and worshipped. Some women attained to special predominance, because they were able to interpret from certain mysterious depths the phenomena of the world. So it came to pass that with these women that which was within them transposed itself into a kind of Nature-speech. For the beginning of speech lies in something akin to song. The power of thought converted itself into that of audible sound. The inner rhythm of Nature resounded through the life of "wise" women. People gathered round such women, and their song-like utterances were felt as the expression of higher powers. Thus did divine worship take its inception among men. It would be an error to consider that there was any "sense" in the spoken word at that time. Only the sound, tone and rhythm were felt. No one had any aim other than that of drawing strength into the soul from what was heard. The whole procedure was under the guidance of the higher leaders. They had inspired the "wise" priestesses with tones and rhythms in a manner which cannot be described publicly, and it was thus that women were able to affect the souls of men in such a way as to ennoble them. It may be said that it was altogether in this manner that the true soul-life was awakened.

The Akashic Records reveal what are in this respect scenes of much beauty. One of these shall be described. We are in a wood close to a gigantic tree. The sun has just risen in the east. Mighty are the shadows thrown by the palm-like tree across the cleared space round it. With her face to the east and in a state of exaltation, we discern a priestess on a seat prepared with curious natural objects and plants. Slowly and in a rhythmic cadence flow from her lips a few wonderful sounds which are repeated again and again. Ranged in large circles, a number of men and women sit round her with dreamy faces, absorbing inner life from the sounds. Still other scenes may be witnessed. At another place, arranged in like manner, a priestess chants in a similar way, but her tones have in them something more mighty,

WOMAN IN THE THIRD ROOT-RACE

more powerful, and the men around her move in rhythmic dances. For this was the other method by means of which the "soul" entered mankind. The mysterious rhythms which man had caught from Nature were imitated in the movements of his own limbs. Thus was it that man felt himself at one with Nature and with the Powers that ruled her.

The part of the earth on which was reared the germ of the coming human race was particularly adapted for this purpose. It was situated where the still agitated and stormy earth had more or less settled down. For Lemuria was greatly troubled by storms. The earth had not then reached its later density. The thin soil was everywhere undermined by volcanic forces bursting forth in smaller or greater streams. Mighty volcanoes were found nearly everywhere and continually exercised a devastating activity. In all their arrangements men were accustomed to take into consideration this fiery agency. They even turned the fire to advantage in respect of their works and enterprises. The state of things was such that this natural fire could be turned to account in human labour just as is the case to-day with artificial fire. It was the activity of volcanic fire that also brought about the ruin of the Lemurian continent. The portion of Lemuria in which the Root-Race of the Atlanteans was to appear had, it is true, a hot climate, but nevertheless was exempt, on the whole, from subjection to the volcanic agency. Human nature could develop itself here more calmly and peacefully. The more nomadic life of former times was abandoned and fixed settlements increased in number.

One has to remember that the human body was at this time still very plastic and flexible. It was still in a state of formation, in keeping with man's inner changes. At a recent era, for instance, men were still quite different as to their external appearance. The external influence of the country and of the climate continued to affect their form. But in the specified colony the body became increasingly an expression of the inner psychic life. This colony contained at the same time a species of men who were advanced and of a finer external form. It should be said that the true human form was created by what had been done by the leaders. The work was certainly very slow and gradual, but the progress began with the unfolding of the psychic life in man; and the still soft and plastic body adapted itself accordingly. It is a law of human development that the transforming influence of man on his physical body decreases with progress. Indeed, this physical body acquired a fairly firm form only through the development of intellectual power, and contemporaneously with the solidification of the stony, mineral and metallic formations of the earth, which were connected with this development. For in the Lemurian, and even also in the Atlantean era, stones and metals were far softer than they afterwards became. This is not in contradiction with the fact that there still exist descendants of the last Lemurians and Atlanteans who even now display forms no less solid than those of the later human races. These remainders had to adapt themselves to the altered conditions surrounding them, and consequently became more rigid. This is precisely the cause of their gradual extinction. They did not mould themselves from within, but their less developed inner nature was forced from without into rigidity and thereby brought to a standstill. And this standstill is truly a retrogression, for even the inner life deteriorated because it could not live itself out in the solidified external body.

Animal life displayed a still greater capacity for change. Reference will be made later on to the kinds of animals present at the time of the earliest races, both as to their origin and also as to the appearance of new forms of animals during the subsequent history of men. Suffice it here to say that the existing animal species were in a state of constant transformation, and that new species continued to arise. This transformation was naturally gradual. The reasons of the transformation lay, partly, in the change of domicile and mode of life. Animals had an extraordinarily quick capacity for adaptation to new conditions. The plastic body altered its organs with comparative quickness, so that, after a longer or shorter time, the descendants of a particular species well nigh ceased to resemble their progenitors. It was also thus with plants, but in a more pronounced degree. The greatest influence on the transformation of man and animals was due to man himself, whether he instinctively brought living beings into such surroundings that they assumed definite forms or whether he attempted to produce changes by breeding. The transforming influence of man on nature was, at that time, incalculably greater than is the case at present, and this was especially the case in the colony described. For here this transformation was guided by the leaders in a manner which was not realized by men. So it came about that, when men went forth to found the various Atlantean races, they took with them highly advanced knowledge as to the breeding of animals and plants. The growth of civilization was then essentially a consequence of the knowledge which they had brought with them. Nevertheless it must be emphasized that these instructions were only instinctive in character and, in essence, they remained so among the first Atlantean races.

The predominance of the woman-soul, already indicated, is particularly strong in the last Lemurian epoch, and continues into the Atlantean era, when the fourth subrace was in preparation. It must not, however, be thought that this was the case with the whole of mankind, but it holds true as regards that portion of the earthly population from which came forth, at a later period, the truly advanced races. This influence was most potent on all that is "unconscious" in man or about him. The acquisition of certain habitual

WOMAN IN THE THIRD ROOT-RACE

gestures, the subtleties of sense perception, the feeling for beauty, a good deal of the sensitive and emotional life common to men in general, emanated originally from the soul of woman. It is not saying too much if we interpret the communications of the Akashic records to this effect: "Civilized nations have a bodily structure and a bodily expression, as well as certain bases of the physically psychic life, which have been stamped on them by woman.

VI

HUMANITY BEFORE THE DIVISION OF SEX

Although the form of man, in those ancient times which have been already described, was very different from his present form, yet, if we go still further back in the history of humanity we find conditions differing even much more widely. For it was only in the course of time that the forms of man and woman arose from an earlier, original form in which the human being was neither the one nor the other, but both at the same time. He who would gain for himself a conception of those primeval ages must free himself entirely from those customary ideas which are drawn from present conditions. The times to which we are looking back lie somewhat before the middle of that epoch called, in the preceding extracts, the Lemurian. The human body then consisted of soft plastic matter; and the rest of the earthly forms also were both soft and plastic. Compared with its later firmness, the earth was still in a bubbling and more fluid state. The human soul, being embodied in that matter, could then adapt itself in a much greater degree than later. For clothing of the soul in a male or female body is due to the fact that the one or the other is forced upon it by the development of external nature. So long as matter had not become firm, the soul could enforce its own laws upon it. It moulded the body in its own likeness; but when matter had grown dense the soul had to suit itself to the laws stamped on this matter by external nature. So long as the soul was master of matter it formed its body neither male nor female, but gave to it qualities common to both. For the soul is at once both male and female. In itself it bears these two natures. Its male element is related to that which we call Will, its female element to what is designated Imagination. The external formation of the earth has led the body to adopt a one-sided evolution. The male body has assumed a form determined by the element of Will; the female, on the contrary, bears rather the impress of Imagination. Thus it is that the bisexual male-female soul inhabits a unisexual male or female body. And so the body had in the course of evolution assumed so decided a form through the influence of external earth-forces that thereafter it was no longer possible for the soul to pour its entire force into this body. It had to retain within itself something of the force that belonged to it, and could allow only a part to flow into the body.

When we study the Akashic Records we see that, at a period in the far past, human forms appear soft, plastic, and quite unlike those of later times. They still retain in equal measure the nature of man and woman. As time passes and matter densifies, the human body appears in two forms, one of which resembles the man's later form, the other the woman's. Before the appearance of these differentiated forms, every human being could of himself bring forth another. The fructification was no outer process, but one which took place within the human body itself. When the body took on a male or a female form, it lost the possibility of self-fructification. Co-operation with another body was necessary in order to produce a new human being.

The separation of the sexes appears when the earth attains a certain condition of density. The density of matter partly checks the power of reproduction, and that portion of the reproductive force which is still effective requires completion from outside by the opposite force in another human being. But the soul must retain within itself a part of its earlier force, in man as well as in woman. It cannot expend this part in the outer corporeal world. Now this portion of his force is directed inwards in man. It cannot appear outwardly; therefore it is set free for the use of inner organs—and here comes an important point in the evolution of mankind. Before it, that which we call mind—the ability to think—could have found no place in man, for this capacity would have had no organ through which to act. The soul turned its whole force outwards to the building up of the body. But now the soul-force, which cannot find an object for its activity without, can unite itself with the mind force, and, by such union, those organs of the body are evolved which, at a later period, make man a thinking being. Thus could man direct a part of the force that in earlier

BEFORE DIVISION OF SEX

times he had turned to the bringing forth of his kind, to the perfecting of his own being. The force by means of which mankind formed for itself a thinking brain, is the same force by which, in ancient times, man fructified himself. Thought is attained by unisexuality. Since man no longer fructifies himself, but the opposite sexes fructify one another, they can turn a part of their productive force inwards and become thinking beings. Thus the male and female bodies respectively present externally an imperfect picture of the soul, but because of this they become inwardly more perfect beings.

Very slowly and gradually this change is accomplished in man. Little by little the later single-sexed human forms appear side by side with those of the double sex.

It is again a kind of fructification which takes place in man on his becoming a thinking being. The inner organs which can be built up by the superfluous soul-force are fructified by the mind. The soul is in itself two-fold: male-female, and so in ancient times it also formed its body. At a later period it can only give to its body a form that can co-operate with another externally; for itself it retains the ability to co-operate with the mind. From this time forward man is fructified from without for the exterior part,—from within and for the interior part of his nature by the mind. It may be said then that the male body has a female soul, the female body a male soul. This inner one-sidedness in man is now balanced by the fructification of the mind. The one-sidedness is removed. The male soul in the female body and the female soul in the male body both become bisexual again through fructification by the mind. Thus do man and woman differ in their outer form, and, within, the one-sidedness of the soul unites itself in both sexes to a harmonious whole. Within, mind and soul melt into unity. The mind affects as female the male soul in woman, and thus makes it male-female; it works upon the female soul in man, as male, and so forms it female-male. The bi-sexuality in man has withdrawn from the outer world, where it existed in pre-Lemurian times, to his inner self.

We see that the higher inner man has nothing to do with male and female. Nevertheless the inner uniformity comes from a male soul in a woman and in like manner from a female soul in a man. The union with the mind brings uniformity at last, but the fact that before the appearance of this uniformity there exists difference—this fact contains a mystery of human nature. The knowledge of this mystery is of great importance to all occult science for it is the key to weighty problems of life. For the present it is forbidden to raise further the veil that covers this mystery.

Thus did physical man develop from the bisexual body to the unisexual,—to the separation into man and woman. And because of this, man has become a being endowed with mentality, such as he now is. But it must not be imagined that there were not intelligent beings in connection with the earth even before this period. If we trace the Akashic Records, we certainly see that in the first Lemurian period the physical man of the future was a very different being from that which we call man to-day. He was unable to connect any sense-perceptions with thoughts: he did not think. His life was one of instinct. His soul expressed itself simply in instincts, desires, animal wishes, and so on. His consciousness was dreamy; he lived in a kind of stupor. But there were other beings in the midst of this humanity. These were of course also bisexual; for with the prevailing conditions in the evolution of the earth at that time, no male or female body could be brought forth. The external conditions were still wanting. But there were other beings who, in spite of their double sex, were able to acquire knowledge and wisdom. This was possible because these beings had undergone an entirely different evolution at a still more remote period of the past. It had become possible for their souls to fertilize themselves with mind without waiting for the development of the inner organs of the human physical body. It is only by the help of the brain that contemporary man is able to ponder upon those impressions which he receives from outside and through the senses. It is the evolution of the soul of man that caused this. The human soul had to wait till there was a brain to co-operate with the mind. The soul would have remained mindless had it not taken this indirect path. It would have remained at the stage of dream-consciousness. It was different with the super-human beings already mentioned. The soul of such beings had developed at earlier stages soul-organs which required nothing physical to enable them to unite themselves with the mind. Their knowledge and wisdom were supersensually acquired. Such knowledge is called intuitive. It is not until a later stage of his evolution that the man of the present attains to this intuition, which enables him to come into touch with mind, apart from the assistance of the senses. He must reach it indirectly through the material senses. This indirect course is called the descent of the human soul into matter, or popularly "The Fall" (into sin). Owing to an earlier evolution of a different kind these superhuman beings did not need to undergo this descent into matter. As the soul of such beings had already attained a higher stage, their consciousness was not dreamy but inwardly luminous, and the comprehension of knowledge and wisdom by them was clairvoyance which needed no senses and no organs of thought. The Wisdom by which the world was built streamed directly into their soul. Thus were they able to be the leaders of young humanity, still sunk in apathy. They were the bearers of an Ancient Wisdom, to comprehend which man must struggle upwards by the roundabout path described. They differed from what is called "man" by the fact that Wisdom poured out its rays on them "from above" as a free gift, just as the sunlight streams down on us. It was not so with "man." He had to acquire wisdom for himself by the labour of the senses and of the organ of thought. It did not at first come to him as a free gift. He must desire it. Only when the longing for wisdom is alive in man, does he strive to attain it for himself through his senses and thought-organ. So a new impulse must awaken in the soul,—desire, the longing for knowledge. The human soul could not possess this longing in its earlier stages. Its impulses were only towards embodiment in that which took on an outer form, in that in which it existed as a dreamy life, but not towards the knowledge of an outer world, not towards understanding. With the separation of the sexes first appeared the desire for knowledge.

It was just because the superhuman beings did not desire it that Wisdom became known to them by the path of clairvoyance. They waited till wisdom streamed into them, as we wait for the sunshine that we cannot create by night, but which must come to us of itself in the morning.

The longing for knowledge is evoked in this way, in order that the soul may build up inner organs (the brain, etc.) by which it comes into possession of knowledge. This result follows because part of the soul-force works no longer from without but from within. But the superhuman beings who have not accomplished this separation of their soul-forces direct their entire soul-energy outwards.

BEFORE DIVISION OF SEX

They have thus also at their service, for the outer fructification by the mind, that force which man turns inwards for the building up of his organs of knowledge. Now that force by means of which man turns outwards to unite himself with another is Love. The superhuman beings directed their whole love outwards to let the wisdom of the worlds stream into their souls. But man can turn outwards only a part. Man became sensual, and thus his love grew sensual too. He withdrew from the outer world the part of his being which he then directed towards his inner building. And this produced what is called "selfishness." When man became man or woman in his physical body, he could only surrender a part of his being; with the other part he separated himself from the surrounding world. He became selfish. And his outer activity as well as his striving for inward development became selfish. He loved, because he desired, and he thought, because again he desired—in this case, knowledge. In contrast to a childish and selfish humanity stood the leaders in their all-loving, unselfish natures. The soul which in them inhabits neither a male nor a female body, is itself male-female. It loves without desire. The innocent soul of man loved thus before the separation of the sexes; nevertheless it could not at that time know, for the very reason that it was still at a lower stage—in dream-consciousness. Thus too does the soul of the higher beings love; nevertheless, these beings can know in spite of this and on acount of their advanced development. "Man" must pass through selfishness in order once more to reach unselfishness at a higher stage, but this time with absolutely clear consciousness.

This, then, was the task of the superhuman beings, of the great leaders,—to stamp upon the young humanity, their own character, that of love. They could do so only with that part of the soul-force which was directed outwards. Thus arose sensual love. And hence the latter accompanies the soul's activity in a male or female body. Sensual love became the force for human physical development. This love brings man and woman together in so far as they are physical beings. On this love rests the progress of physical humanity. It was over this love only that the so-called superhuman beings had power. That part of the human soul-force which turns inwards and must gain knowledge by the indirect path of sensuality, withdraws itself from the power of those superhuman beings. They themselves had never descended to the development of corresponding inner organs. They could clothe the outward impulse in love, because they possessed as their very essense the love that was outwardly active. Thus there was a gulf between them and the young humanity. They could implant love in man, at first in a sensual form; knowledge they could not give because their own knowledge had never taken the by-path through those inner organs which man was now developing in himself. They could

BEFORE DIVISION OF SEX

speak no language which a being with brains could understand.

Now the said inner organs of man were, it is true, not ripe for contact with mind till that stage of earthly existence was reached which lies in the middle of the Lemurian period; but once before, at a much earlier period of development, they had been cultivated into an imperfect first beginning. For the soul had already passed through physical embodiments in times long gone by. It had lived, not indeed on the earth, but on other celestial bodies in densified matter. More exact information on this subject cannot be given till later. Only so much as this may now be said,—the beings of earth had formerly inhabited another planet, and, according to the conditions existing on it, they had developed to the stage at which they stood when they reached the earth. They laid aside the matter of the preceding planet like a garment, and became pure soul-germs at the stage of development reached then, —capable of sensation, of feeling, and so on; in short, able to lead that dreamlike life which still belonged to them in the first stages of their earth existence. But the superhuman beings spoken of, the leaders in the domain of love, had also lived on the preceding planets, and were even there so perfect that they no longer needed to descend in order to develop the first beginnings of those inner organs. But there were other beings, not so far advanced as these Leaders of Love, but who might rather be counted as men on the preceding planet, who nevertheless outstripped mankind at that time. They were thus indeed, at the beginning of the earth formation, further advanced than man, but nevertheless still at the stage at which knowledge must be acquired through inner organs. These beings were in a peculiar position. They were too far advanced to pass through the physical human body, either male or female, and yet not far enough to be able to act by means of perfect clairvoyance as were the Leaders of Love. They could not be, as yet, *Beings of Love,* and at the same time they could no longer be "men." So it was only possible for them as semi-superhuman beings to continue their own evolution, but with the help of man. They could converse with the beings with brains in a language understood by the latter. By this means the human soul-force directed inwards was aroused, and they could unite themselves to knowledge and wisdom. It was only thus indeed that wisdom of a human sort came to the earth. The "semi-superhuman beings" spoken of were able to absorb this human wisdom, and thus themselves reach that which they still lacked of perfection. They thus became the creators of human wisdom. For this reason they were called "light bringers" (Lucifer). Thus had infant humanity leaders of two kinds—Beings of Love and Beings of Wisdom,—human nature was yoked between Love and Wisdom, when it assumed its present form on the earth. By the Beings of Love it was stimulated to physical development, by the Beings of Wisdom to the perfection of its inner self. In consequence of its physical development, mankind advanced from generation to generation, forming new tribes and races; through its inner development, the individuals increased in inward perfection; they became scholars, sages, artists, technical scientists, etc. From race to race physical humanity advances; each race throughout its physical evolution transfers to the following one, such of its qualities as are perceptible to the senses. Here the law of heredity reigns. The children bear the physical characteristics of the fathers. Beyond this lies an evolution towards perfection of mind and soul which can only be accomplished by the development of the soul itself. And here we are confronted with the law of the evolution of the soul within the bounds of earthly existence.

VII

THE BEGINNINGS OF SEX DUALITY

A description of the constitution of man before the division into male and female sexes must now be given. The body consisted then of a soft, plastic mass. Over it the will-power was far more potent than in the case of subsequent mankind. On his separation from the parent being, man appeared, it is true, as an organism with members, but incomplete. His organs continued their further development apart from the parent body. Much of that which at a later period ripened within the maternal organism was then brought to perfection by an external force akin to our will-power. The parent's fostering care was necessary to promote such a ripening from without. Man brought with him into the world certain organs which he afterwards discarded. Others, still quite imperfect at his first appearance, completed their development. The whole process permits of a comparison with liberation from an egg-form, and the casting off of an outer covering; but one must not here think of a hard and egg-like shell.

Man's body was warm-blooded. This must be distinctly stated, for in former times it was otherwise, as will afterwards be shown. The process of maturing apart from the mother-entity was accomplished under the influence of increased warmth, conveyed in like manner from without. But by no means must one imagine a *hatching-out* of the egg-shaped man—so named for the sake of brevity. The conditions of warmth and fire on the earth were different then from those of later times. By means of his own force a man could constrain and confine into a certain space fire or warmth. In a phrase, he could concentrate heat. He was thus in a position to supply warmth to the young creature that required it for his development.

The motory organs were at that time man's most highly developed organs. The sense organs of to-day were then quite unevolved. The most advanced were the organ of hearing and the organs for the perception of cold and heat (the sense of feeling); still far behind was the perception of light. Man was born with the senses of hearing and of touch and then, somewhat later, the light-perception was evolved.

All that is stated here refers to the latest period before the separation of the sexes. The latter proceeded slowly and gradually. For a long time before its actual appearance, mankind began to develop in such a way that one individual was born with more of the masculine, the other with more of the feminine character. Nevertheless, the characteristics of the opposite sex were present in every individual, so that spontaneous generation was possible, though not at all times, for it was dependant upon the influences of external conditions at certain seasons of the year. In divers matters mankind as a whole depended to a large extent on such external circumstances. For that reason he had to regulate all his undertakings in accordance with such outer conditions; in accordance, for example, with the course of sun and moon. This regulation did not, however, take place consciously, in the present sense of the term, but was carried out in a manner which must rather be called instinctive, and by that term the mental life of the man of that time has been indicated.

This mental life cannot be described as an actual inner life. Bodily and mental activities and qualities were not as yet separated rigidly from one another. The outer life of Nature was still experienced by the soul. It was above all on the sense of hearing that every single vibration from without made a powerful impression. Every quiver in the air, every movement in his surroundings was "heard." The wind and the water expressed in their motions what to man was an "eloquent language." It was a perception of the mysterious weaving and working in Nature which thus penetrated man. And this weaving and working resounded again in his soul. His activity was an echo of these influences. He transformed the perception of sound into his own activity. He lived amid those surgings of sound, and brought them into expression by means of his own will. In like manner he was impelled to accomplish all his daily work. To a somewhat less degree, indeed, he was affected by the energy playing upon his feelings. Nevertheless these too acted an important part. The surroundings were sensed by him within his own body and he acted accordingly. By the activities of his feelings he knew when and how he ought to work. By these he knew where to settle, or recognized the dangers threatening his life, and so avoided them. He regulated the taking of sustenance accordingly.

Altogether different from that of later times was the course taken by the rest of his mental life. Pictures lived in his soul, but not as representations of external things. When, for example, the man moved from a colder into a warmer place, there arose in his soul a definite colour-picture, but this colour-picture had nothing to do with any external object. It sprang from an inner force akin to the will. Pictures like these continually filled the soul. The whole can only be compared with the rising and falling dream-visions of man. Only at that time the pictures were not unregulated, but were in conformity with law, and for that reason we must speak, not of a dream-consciousness at this stage of humanity, but rather of a picture-consciousness. In the main it was colour-pictures with which this consciousness was filled, but these were not the only kind. Thus man wandered through the world, experiencing its events by means of his senses of hearing and feeling; but in his inner life this world was reflected in pictures, very unlike those existing in the outer world.

BEGINNINGS OF SEX DUALITY

Pleasure and pain were bound up with these soul-pictures in a much smaller degree than is the case with man's ideas to-day, which reflect his perceptions in the world outside. Doubtless one picture caused him pleasure, another disgust, the one hatred, and the other love; but these sensations bore a much fainter character. On the other hand strong feelings were produced by something else. Man was then much more agile, much more active than later. Everything in his surroundings, as well as the pictures in his soul, stirred him to activity, to movement. Now when his activity, unhindered, had free play, he experienced a sensation of well-being; when, however, this activity was checked in any direction, he was overcome by unhappiness and discomfort. The absence or presence of opposition to his will determined the content of his life of feeling, his pleasure and his pain. And this pleasure or this pain discharged itself again in his own soul as a living world of pictures. Clear, bright, beautiful pictures lived within him when he was able to expand unhindered; gloomy and misshapen were those which appeared in his soul when his movements were hampered.

So far the average man has been described. In the case of those who had developed into a a kind of superhuman state the inner life was different. With them the soul life was not of this instinctive character. What they perceived through their senses of hearing and of feeling were Nature's deeper secrets, and these they could consciously interpret.

In the roaring of the wind, in the rustling of the trees, the laws and the wisdom of Nature were disclosed, and in their soul-pictures these were not mere reflections of an outer world, but images of the spiritual powers in the world. It was not the things of sense which they perceived, but spiritual intelligences. If the average man, for example, experienced a sensation of fear, a hideous sinister picture would arise in his soul. The superhuman being received by means of such pictures information, revelation from the spiritual beings of the world. The processes of Nature did not appear to him as they do to the naturalist of to-day, dependent on lifeless natural laws, but rather as the deeds of spiritual beings. The outer reality did not as yet exist, for there were no outer senses, but to the higher beings the inner reality revealed itself. The spirit poured its rays into them as the sunlight streams into the physical eye of the man of today. In these beings was knowledge in its fullest sense, that which is called intuitive knowledge. There was no such thing as combining and speculating among them, but a direct contemplation of the working of spiritual beings. These superhuman individualities could thus absorb directly, into their wills, communications coming from the spiritual world. Consciously they led the others. They received their mission from the spiritual world and acted in accordance with it.

Now when the time arrived at which the sexes separated, these

BEGINNINGS OF SEX DUALITY

beings naturally considered it their task to influence the new life in agreement with their mission. The regulation of sexual life originated with them. All arrangements which had to do with the generation of mankind had their source in them. In this they acted with perfect consciousness, but the other human beings were sensible of the impulse only as an instinct impanted in them. Sexual love was implanted in man by direct thought-transference; and all its expressions were at first of the noblest kind. Everything in this domain which has taken on an ugly character dates from a later period when man had become more independent, and when he had sullied a desire originally pure. In these early times there was no such thing as a satisfaction of sexual desire for its own sake. Everything then was a service of sacrifice for the continuance of human existence. Generation was regarded as a sacred thing, as a service which man owed to the world, and sacrificial priests were the leaders and rulers in this domain.

Of another kind were the influences of the semi-superhuman beings. The latter were not developed to the stage at which they could receive the revelations of the spiritual world in all their purity. In their soul-pictures there arose, besides the impressions of the spiritual world the activities also of the world of sense. Those who were in the fullest sense superhuman beings had no sensation of either pleasure or pain from the external world. They abandoned themselves entirely to the revelations of the spiritual powers. Wisdom flowed into them as light flows into the creatures of sense. Their will was directed towards nothing else but to action in accordance with this wisdom, and in action of this kind lay their highest pleasure. Wisdom, Will, and Activity composed their very being. It was otherwise with the semi-superhuman beings. They felt the desire to receive impressions from without, and connected pleasure with the satisfaction of this desire, disappointment with its non-satisfaction. They were thus distinguishable from the superhuman beings. For the latter, impressions from without were nothing more than confirmation of spiritual revelations. They might behold the outer world and receive nothing more than a reflection of that which they had already received through the spirit. The semi-superhuman beings experienced something new to them, and on that account *they* were able to be the leaders of mankind, when the latter began to change the mere pictures in the soul into images, into representations of outer objects. This happened when a part of the earlier human generative force turned inwards and when beings possessing a brain were evolved. For with the brain man also developed the capacity to change external sense-impressions into mind-conceptions. It must be said therefore that man was impelled by semi-superhuman beings to turn his soul towards the external world of sense. It was indeed denied him to expose his own soul pictures directly to pure spiritual

BEGINNINGS OF SEX DUALITY

influences. The ability to generate his kind was implanted in him as an instinctive impulse by the superhuman beings. Mentally he would have had to lead a sort of dream-existence at first, had not the semi-superhuman beings interfered. Swayed by them his soul-pictures were directed to the world outside. He became a being self-conscious in the world of sense. And thus man achieved the ability to guide his actions consciously and according to his perceptions in the world of sense. Once he had acted from a kind of instinct, under the sway of his external surroundings and the energizing forces playing upon him from higher individualities. Now he began to follow the urgings, the allurements, of his own conceptions. And with this the free will of mankind appeared in the world. That was the beginning of "Good and Evil."

Before advancing farther in this direction something must be said about man's environment on the earth. Side by side with man there existed animals as well, which according to their kind were at the same stage of development as he was. In accordance with our present conceptions they would be counted as reptiles. Besides these there were lower forms of the animal world. Now there was an essential difference between man and the animals. On account of his still plastic body, man could only live in those regions of the earth which had not as yet reached the densest material form, and in these regions animals possessing a like plastic body lived with him. In other regions however animals

BEGINNINGS OF SEX DUALITY

lived which had already dense bodies and which had also already developed unisexuality and their sense organs. Whence they came will be shown later. They could develop no farther because their bodies had taken on the denser matter too soon. Some species among them have disappeared, some have developed further after their kind into the present forms. Man was able to reach higher forms because he remained in those regions which suited his structure at that time. On that account his body remained so flexible and soft that he was able to single out of himself those organs which were capable of fructification by the mind. His external body had then advanced so far that it could densify, and become a protecting sheath for the finer mental organs.

But all human bodies were not so far developed. Those that were so advanced were few. These were first of all vivified by the mind. Others were not vivified. Had the mind entered the latter as well, it would only have been able partially to evolve, because of the imperfect inner organs. And so these human personalities had for the time being to continue their development as a kind of mindless creature. A third kind had proceeded so far that feeble mental impulses could make themselves felt. These stood between the other two kinds. Their mental activity remained dull. They had to be led by higher mental powers. Between these three kinds were all possible grades of transition. Further development was now only possible if one part of mankind should educate itself more

BEGINNINGS OF SEX DUALITY

highly at the cost of another part. First of all, the absolutely mindless had to be sacrificed. An intermingling with them for the purpose of propagation would only have dragged the more advanced down to their level. And so all who had received the mind principle were singled out from among them. Therefore they fell more and more to the level of animality. Thus, side by side with mankind, animals resembling man evolved themselves further. Man left, as it were, a portion of his brothers behind him on the path, so that he might himself mount higher. This process was however by no means at an end here. Those men also of dull mentality, who stood rather higher, could only advance further by being drawn into association with higher beings and by separating themselves from the less mentally gifted. Only by these means could they develop bodies afterwards suited for the reception of the entire human intelligence. Not until after the lapse of a certain time had physical evolution advanced so far that, in this direction, a sort of pause set in, during which all lying beyond a fixed limit belonged to the human domain. The conditions of life on the earth had meantime so changed that a further rejection would have resulted in the production, not of animal-like beings, but of such as were not even fit to live. But what was thrust down into a state of animality has either died out or lives on in the various higher animals. In such, therefore, we must recognize creatures which had to remain behind, at an earlier stage of human development. Only they have not retained the same form which they had at the time of their separation, but have degenerated from a higher to a lower type. Thus monkeys are retrograde human beings of a by-gone age. Just as man was at one time less perfect than he is to-day, so were these at one time more perfect than at present. And that which remained within the domain of man has undergone a like process, within its own limits. In many a savage tribe we may see the degraded descendants of human forms which were at one time more exalted. These have not sunk to the level of the brute, but only to that of the savage.

That which in man is eternal is the mind. It has been shown at what period the mind entered the body. Before that time the mind belonged to other regions. It could not unite itself with the body till the latter had attained a certain stage of development. Only when there is a perfect comprehension of the way in which this union took place can the meaning of birth and death be understood, or the character of the everlasting mind be known.

VIII

MAN'S FIRST ANCESTORS

The observations of the Akashic Records which will be described in the following pages, date from a period immediately preceding the incidents related in the previous chapter. In view of the materialistic tendency of thought at the present day, the risk attending the publication of the following facts is even greater than that incurred by the descriptions given in the preceding chapters. One is so liable in these days, when dealing with matters of this kind, to be dubbed fantastic, or accused of groundless speculation. Nothing but the conviction that the information we offer with regard to spiritual experience is true and accurate, could induce us to publish these statements, knowing, as we do only too well, that any one who is versed in the teachings of Physical Science as accepted by the present generation, will be unable even to approach the matter in a serious attitude of mind. Nothing is here stated, but that which has been carefully tested according to the methods employed by Spiritual Science; and all we ask of the ordinary scientist is that he shall accord to the student of the Higher Science the same toleration as the latter shows to the mode of thought of Physical Science. (See my "Welt- und Lebensanschauungen im Neunzehnten Jahrhundert," where I think I have shown my appreciation of the views held by materialistic Science).

Nevertheless, for the benefit of any who may be sympathetically inclined towards the teachings of the Higher Science, I would add a further special remark with reference to the present expositions. We shall here touch upon matters of very great significance, pertaining to an age now long past, matters which, portrayed by the Records of Akasha, it is by no means an easy task to decipher. The writer, indeed, makes no claim on blind faith; he merely sets forth the results of investigations on which the utmost care has been bestowed. Any correction, if based on a practical knowledge of such matters, would be welcomed. The signs of the times are such as to impress him with a sense of duty, nay, urgency, in making known these events in the evolution of mankind. Moreover, we shall first have to sketch briefly an extensive period of existence, in order to gain at the outset a good general idea. Many things, therefore, which are now merely indicated, will receive a more detailed exposition in later chapters.

It is, however, difficult to translate the inscriptions of the Akashic Record into every-day language. It were easier to decipher the occult language of symbolic signs used in occult schools, but this is not yet permitted in our time. The reader is therefore begged to give a hearing to much that may seem obscure and hard to understand; to make a valiant endeavor to grasp their meaning, as the author, on his part, has striven to devise a mode of representation capable of being understood by all. The trouble expended in mastering many a difficult passage will be rewarded by the insight gained into the profound mysteries, the momentous problems of humanity herein revealed. These Akashic Records, which for the occult investigator are as much an undeniable reality as mountains and rivers are for the physical eye, constitute the basis of a true knowledge of self for man. An error of perception is, of course, possible for the one as for the other.

It must be remembered that the present chapter relates only to the evolution of man. As a matter of course, the other kingdoms of Nature, the mineral, the plant and the animal, are evolving side by side with humanity, and these other evolutions will be dealt with in future chapters. In these we shall discuss certain other subjects destined to illumine and to render more comprehensible the details given concerning man's evolution. On the other hand, we shall not be able to study the evolution of the other terrestrial kingdoms from the occult standpoint until the gradual development of man has been shown.

When we retrace still further the earth's evolutionary history,—further back even than we have done in the foregoing pages,—we find our celestial globe composed of ever finer conditions of matter. The matter which later became solid was, at a previous stage, liquid; before that, gaseous and of the nature of vapour; while at a still remoter period, we find it in its finest form, that is to say, as ether.

MAN'S FIRST ANCESTORS

The decrease of temperature, however, caused the gradual solidification of matter.

In our present studies we shall go back to the time when our earthly dwelling-place was composed of matter in its finest etheric state. In that epoch of the earth's evolution, man began his earthly career. In earlier times he had lived in other worlds, which will be the subject of study elsewhere.* We will here only say a word or two about the existence which immediately preceded his earth-life. It was what we should call an astral or spiritual world, peopled with beings who had no outer, that is to say, no physical, corporeal existence. Neither had man. He had

---

* See "An Outline of Occult Science," by Rudolf Steiner, Ph.D.

by that time perfected the picture-consciousness, or dream-consciousness, which was described in a foregoing chapter. He possessed feelings and desires, but all confined in a soul-body: a human being at that stage would only have been visible to clairvoyant sight.

It is true that the more highly evolved human beings of that period possessed such sight, though it was of a rather vague and dreamy description; it was *not* self-conscious clairvoyance. These astral beings are, in a certain sense, man's ancestors; for what to-day we call "Man" contains an indwelling, self-conscious Spirit. This Spirit became united to the being which descended from that ancestor about the middle of the Lemurian phase of civilisation. (This union of the Soul-Ancestor with the

Physical-Ancestor has already been mentioned in earlier chapters. The subject will be taken up again, and treated more explicitly, after we have followed the evolution of man's ancestors up to that point.)

The astral or Soul-Ancestors of man were transplanted to the subtle matter of the etheric world. They absorbed this subtle matter into themselves,—roughly putting it—something after the manner of a sponge. Thus, by permeating themselves with etheric matter their etheric bodies were formed. They were elongated and elliptic in form; yet subtle differentiations of matter, tendencies to form limbs and other organs to be developed at a later period, were even then perceptible. The whole process perceptible in the mass of etheric matter was, however, purely physiochemical, though regulated and controlled by the soul.

When one of these ovoids of matter had reached a certain size it split into two, forming two new masses each resembling the one which gave it birth, and reproducing the same activities which were at work in the parent form. Every one of these new forms possessed a soul similar to that of the mother-being. The reason of this was that not only a definite number of human souls incarnated on the physical plane, but there was what we might call a Soul-Tree (or Group Soul), which was able, as it were, to give off innumerable individual souls, sprung from its common root. Just as a plant springs up again and again from numberless seeds, so did the soul-life reincarnate in the countless offshoots which were created as the result of these continual cleavings. (Of course, there existed from the beginning a very limited number of soul species, but within these species, evolution proceeded in the manner described, every soul species putting forth innumerable sprouts).

With incarnation in physical matter a most important change came over the souls themselves. As long as the souls remained unconnected with the material world, no outward material occurrence could affect them. All influences affecting them were purely psychic, or clairvoyant. Thus in their life they shared the astral influences of their surroundings, and it was in this way that they took part in, or experienced, everything that existed at that time. The impressions made by stones, plants, and animals, then also existing in a purely astral (soul) form, were felt as inner experiences of the soul. On entering the plane of our earth, something quite new was added. Outer material events brought influences to bear upon the soul, which had thus robed itself in a garment of etheric matter. At first these influences consisted of motions in the outer material world which caused corresponding activity in the etheric body. In the same way as the vibrations of the air now affect us in the form of sound, so were those etheric beings affected by the vibrations of the etheric matter surrounding them. Such a being was, in fact, a single organ of hearing. This sense was the first to be developed; but from this we see that the separated organ of hearing was formed at a later period.

With the increasing solidification of physical matter, the soul-nature gradually lost control over its formation. The bodies already formed could only reproduce bodies after their own image. A change now occurs in the manner of generation, that is to say, the offspring of the mother-being appears considerably smaller, only growing gradually to the size of the parent. Organs of generation now begin to appear, whereas hitherto they had not existed. Henceforward it is no mere physico-chemical process which takes place within the form. Such a process is now no longer sufficient for the purpose of generation, for the outer matter, growing denser and denser, is no longer capable of being directly influenced by the soul. A special portion within the form is therefore

ATLANTIS AND LEMURIA

set apart for this function, being withdrawn from the immediate influence of the outside material world. Only the body exclusive of the specialized part, is still exposed to these influences; and it remains in the condition which was formerly that of the whole body. In the specialised part the psychic nature continues to work, and the soul becomes at this point the vehicle of the life-principle (called in Theosophical literature 'Prana').

We now find the physical human ancestor in possession of two principles: one being the physical body, which is subject to the chemical and physical laws of the world surrounding it; and the second, the sum total of the organs directly controlled by the individual life-principle. In this manner, a part of the activity of the soul has been liberated. No longer retaining power over the physical sheath, the soul turns this part of its activity inwards, transforming part of the body into special organs; and so begins an inner life of the body. It no longer merely participates in the vibrations from without, but begins to feel them inwardly as individual experiences. Here sensation begins. At first, the sensation somewhat resembles the sense of touch: the subject *feels* the movements of the outer world, the pressure caused by substances, and so on; also the beginnings of a sensation of heat and cold was now developed.

At this point man has reached an important stage in his evolution. The direct influence of the soul has been withdrawn from the physical body, the latter being entirely surrendered to the physical and chemical activities of the material world. The moment the soul, at work in the other principles, relaxes its hold over the body, the latter dissolves. This is the beginning of what we call "death." We cannot speak of death in reference to previous states. In the simple case of separation, the life of the mother-form is continued in the offspring, for in the latter are at work all the transformed soul forces which hitherto had sought expression in the one parent-form; after the separation, nothing remains that is soul-less.

A change now takes place: as soon as the soul ceases to retain its power over the physical body, the latter is subject to the chemical and physical laws of the outer world, that is to say, it decays.

MAN'S FIRST ANCESTORS

The field of activity for the soul-powers is limited to generation and the developed inner life; for through this generative power, descendants are brought forth, which are in their turn endowed with a surplus of organ-forming power. In this surplus the soul always returns to life again. As the whole body was formerly filled with psychic activity at the separation, so were now the organs of reproduction and of sensation. We must recognize in this nothing less than a *Re-birth* of the soul-life in the new growing organism.

Theosophical literature describes these two evolutionary stages of man as the first two Root-Races of our earth. The first is called the Polar Race, the second the Hyperborean Race.

We must bear in mind that the

field of sensation possessed by these human forefathers, was of a general character and as yet quite vague and indefinite. So far, only two of the kinds of sensation we now possess were differentiated: the sense of hearing and that of touch. By reason of the changes, however, which the body was undergoing, as well as its physical environment, the whole human form was no longer capable of acting, so to speak, as "all ear." Henceforward a specialised part of the body retained the power of responding to the delicate vibrations, and supplied the material from which was gradually developed the organ of hearing we now possess, whilst the rest of the body remined almost entirely an organ of touch.

Obviously, the whole process of

the evolution of man has hitherto been connected with the alteration in the degree of warmth of our earth; it was, in fact, due to the heat in his surroundings that man evolved to the stage we have just described. The heat from without, however, had now reached a point at which further progress in the formation of the human body was no longer possible. Thus, with the cooling off of the earth, a corresponding reaction set in within the form itself, and man became the generator of his own supply of heat, whereas hitherto his temperature had been that of his surroundings. Organs now appear in him, enabling him to generate for himself the degree of heat necessary for his life. Up till now, currents of substances had circulated within him, dependent on the environment for the necessary heat; but now he could generate his own heat for these substances, and the fluids of the body turned into warm blood. Thus he had attained a far greater degree of self-dependence as a physical being than ever before, and his whole inner life was intensified. Sensation still depended entirely upon the effects of the outer world. The filling of the body with its own warmth gave it an independent physical inner life. The soul had now a field of activity within the body, where it could unfold an existence which would no longer be a mere sharing in the life of the outer world.

By this proceeding the astral, or soul life, was drawn into the sphere of physical matter. Hitherto desires, longings and passions, joy and sorrow of soul, could only arise through psychic influences; and attraction and aversion were awakened, passions excited, and so on, by that which proceeded from one soul to another. No other external physical object could have produced such effects. Now, for the first time, the possibility arose that such outer objects had a significance for the soul. For the quickening of the inner life which followed the power of generating its own heat caused it to experience the sensation of pleasure, while the disturbance of this inner life caused it discomfort: an outer object qualified to maintain bodily comfort could become an object of desire, or longing. The astral, or desire body,—known as "Kama" in Theosophical literature,—was united with terrestrial man, and the objects of the senses became objects capable of being desired; man was thus bound through his desire body to earthly existence.

The foregoing fact coincides with a great cosmic event, with which it is causally connected. Till now there had been no material separation between sun, earth and moon: these three affected man as a single body. At this point separation occurs: the finer matter, including all that which had hitherto conferred on the soul the power of directly giving life, was separated off as Sun; the grossest matter went forth as Moon; while the earth, with its materiality, occupied a position between the two. Of course, the separation did not occur suddenly; for the whole process was gradually taking place while man was advancing from the stage of generation by cleavage to that just described. The advance in man's evolution was, indeed, accomplished just through the cosmic happenings mentioned. First, the sun withdrew its substance from the common globe. The soul was thereby deprived of the possibility of directly vivifying the earth substance left behind. Then the moon began to take form, in this way bringing about a condition of the earth favourable to the growth of the capacity for sensation just as we have already described.

In conjunction with this occurrence, a new sense was developed. The conditions of warmth of the earth became such that the bodies gradually took on a definite outline, dividing the transparent matter from the opaque. The sun, which had withdrawn from the earth body, now assumed its task as light-giver, and awoke in the human body the sense of sight. It was not at first what we know as sight to-day. Light and darkness were perceptible to man as vague sensations. For instance, he was aware that under certain conditions light gave him a sense of comfort and well-being, quickening the life in his body, therefore he sought it and strove towards it.

Meanwhile the actual soul-life continued to run its course in the form of dreamlike pictures. Colour-pictures came and went in this life, without having any particular connection with the things of the outer world, and these colour-pictures were still attributed by man to soul activities. Light colour-pictures appeared to him when his astral experiences were pleasant; sombre pictures when he was affected by disagreeable astral influences. That which was effected as the result of self-generated heat, we have called in the foregoing the "inner life." Nevertheless, we see that it was not an inner life in the sense of later human development. All things advance step by step, and so does the evolution of the inner life. In the sense in which it has been spoken of in a former chapter, this true inner life only begins when the fructification by the mind takes place, when man begins to think about these outer influences. All that has been described here does but show how man climbed upward to the state depicted in the preceding chapter. And we really live over again the times there described, when we picture to ourselves the following. More and more the soul learns to relate to the outer bodily existence that which it formerly lived through in itself and which it only attributed to soul influences.

The same thing now happened with regard to the colour-pictures. Just as before the impression of a sympathetic psychic influence was connected in the individual soul with a bright colour-picture, so now in a brilliant light-impression from outside the soul began to perceive in colours the objects surrounding it. This was in conjunction with the development of new organs of sight. In its previous stages, the body had one eye, which does not exist to-day, by means of which it vaguely sensed the light and the darkness. (The Legend of the Cyclops with one eye is a reminiscence of this state).

The two eyes developed when the soul began to associate the external light-impressions more intimately with its own life; and thus was lost the capacity of perception of the surrounding astral world. The soul became more and more a mirror of the outer world, the latter being reproduced within it as an image; and simultaneously with this, the separation of the sexes appeared. On the one hand, the human body became capable of fecundation only by another human being, while on the other hand there developed in the body 'soul-organs' (the nervous system), by which the sense-impressions of the outer world were reflected in the soul, thereby preparing the way for the mind, or thinking principle, in the human body.

IX

THE FIRST, OR POLAR, RACE

We will now trace the Akashic Records back to the primeval past, when our earth, as it is now, began to exist. By earth we mean that condition of our planet by reason of which it is the bearer of minerals, plants, animals and men, in their present form; for this state was preceded by others in which the above-named kingdoms of Nature existed under essentially different forms.

The earth, as we know it, had undergone many transformations before it could become the bearer of our present world of minerals, plants, animals and human beings. Minerals also existed in those earlier conditions, but they had quite a different appearance from the minerals of our day. These past conditions will be dealt with later, but for the time being we shall merely refer to the way in which the condition immediately preceding the present was transformed into the latter.

We may form a faint idea of such a transformation by comparison with the passage of the plant nature through the germinal state. Imagine a plant with its roots, stem, leaves, blossoms and fruit: it draws matter from its surroundings and expels it again. But everything belonging to it of the nature of substance, form and growth, disappears—all but the tiny germ; through it the life quickens, to spring up again next year in a similar form. In the same way, all that existed on our earth in its previous state disappeared, but only to arise again in its present form. That which might be called mineral, plant, animal, in the former condition, has passed away, as the roots, stem, and different parts of the plant have passed away; and in one case as in the other, the germ-state has remained out of which the old form is built up anew, for within the germ lie concealed the forces which cause the new form to proceed from it.

In the period which we are just about to describe, we have to deal, therefore, with a kind of earth-germ, containing within it the forces which gave rise to the earth of to-day, forces which were acquired by virtue of its former conditions. We must not imagine, however, that this earth-seed consisted of dense matter like the plant-seed: it was rather of a psychic nature, and composed of that fine, vibrating, plastic matter which is called "astral" in Theosophical literature.

This astral germ of the earth at first contained the embryonic human being, the beginnings of the future human souls. Everything which existed in previous states as minerals, plants and animals, had been absorbed by these human germs—merged in them. So, before man trod the physical earth, he was a soul—an astral being,—and as such he finds himself on the physical earth, which then consisted of the finest matter,—called in Theosophical literature, the finest etheric matter.

The origin of this etheric earth

THE FIRST, OR POLAR, RACE

will be explained in another chapter. The astral human beings drew this ether round them, imprinting on it, as it were, their own nature, so that it became a copy of the astral human being. Thus, in the first stage, we have to deal with an etheric earth, which is really only composed of this etheric humanity, and is nothing but a conglomerate of it. The astral body, or soul of man, is actually, for the most part, outside the etheric body and organises it from without. To the occult investigator the earth appears somewhat as follows: it is a sphere composed in its turn of countless tiny etheric spheres—etheric humanity—and surrounded by an astral covering, as the present earth is surrounded by a covering of air. In this astral envelope (atmosphere) astral humanity lives, and from there it works on its etheric images. The astral human souls create organs in their etheric images, in whom they effect a human etheric existence. Within the whole earth there is only one condition of matter, and that is the subtle vital ether. This primeval humanity is called in Theosophical books the Polar, or First Root-Race.

The further evolution of the earth now consists in the development of the one condition of matter into two; a denser matter separates off, leaving a finer substance behind. The denser substance is similar to our air, while the finer substance resembles that which effects the formation of chemical elements from their previously undifferentiated substance. In addition to these, a remnant of the earlier matter—the vitalised ether—continued

THE FIRST, OR POLAR, RACE

to exist. Only a part of the latter was incorporated with the two conditions of matter just described.

We find, then, at this time three kinds of matter in the physical earth. While formerly the activities of the astral human beings were confined to one substance in the earth-shell, they now had to work upon three, their work being carried on in the following manner. That part which had become gaseous at first offered resistance to the work of the astral beings; it would not assimiliate all the latent possibilities contained in the perfect astral beings; consequently, the astral humanity is forced to divide into two groups. One group is that which elaborates the gaseous matter, and creates in it its own image; the other group is able to do more; it can work upon the two other kinds of matter; it can create an image of itself composed both of the vitalised ether and the other kind of ether, thus giving rise to the chemical elements. In the present work we shall call this kind of ether "chemical-ether."

But this second group of astral beings has only acquired this higher faculty by throwing off a part—the first group— of the astral essence, and condemning it to perform lower work. Had it retained in itself those forces which accomplished the meaner task, it could not have risen higher itself. Here we have an event arising from the fact that something higher procures its own advancement at the cost of another, which it severs from itself.

This is the picture which now presents itself within the physical earth: two kinds of beings exist. Firstly, those having a gaseous body, on which astral beings belonging to it work from outside. These beings are of the nature of animals, and form a first animal kingdom on the earth. Were we to describe the forms of these animals, the man of to-day would think them rather strange. Their form—we must bear in mind that it consisted only of gaseous substance—resembles none of the animal forms existing now; they have, perhaps, a distant resemblance to the shells of certain snails or shell-fish of the present day.

Side by side with these animal forms, man's physical development progresses. Astral humanity, now risen a step higher, creates a physical image of itself consisting of two kinds of matter, of vital ether and of chemical ether. Thus we have before us a human being consisting of an astral body, who is working upon an etheric body, which is again composed of two kinds of ether, vital and chemical ether.

By means of the life-ether this physical image of man has the power of reproduction, of bringing forth beings like itself. By means of the chemical-ether, it develops certain forces, similar to the chemical forces known to us at the present day as attraction and repulsion. Thereby this human image has the power of attracting certain substances in its surroundings and of uniting them with itself,—afterwards to throw them out again by the power of repulsion. Such matter can, of course, only be drawn from the animal kingdom described above and from the human kingdom. Here we discover the origin of nutrition. These first images were thus animal and man-eaters. There still existed simultaneously with these the descendants of the former, merely life-ether beings, but they became stunted, having to adapt themselves to the new terrestrial conditions. From these are formed at a later period, after many transformations undergone by them, the unicellular creatures, as also the cells which afterwards went to the formation of the more complicated beings.

The next step forward is this: the gaseous matter divides in two, the denser part becoming watery and the other remaining gaseous. But the chemical ether also divides into two conditions of matter; the one becomes denser, and forms what we shall here call light-ether; it confers on the beings in whom it is contained the gift of becoming luminous. But a part of the chemical ether retains its original form. We have henceforth to deal with a physical earth composed of the following kinds of matter: water, air, light-ether, chemical-ether and life-ether. Now, to enable the astral beings to influence these kinds of matter again, another occurrence takes place, involving the progress of something higher at the expense of something lower thrown off from it. This process gives rise to physical beings of the character we shall now describe.

Firstly, there were those whose physical body was made up of water and air, who are now worked upon by coarse astral beings belonging to those who had been thrown out. So there arises a new group of animals composed of denser matter than the former ones. Secondly, another new group of physical beings came into existence, possessing a body which may consist of air and light-ether mixed with water. These are plant-like beings, but differing greatly in form from the plants of the present time. Only in the third new group do we find the man of that time represented. His physical body is composed of three kinds of ether, light-ether, chemical-ether and life-ether. When we consider that descendants of the old groups still continue to exist, we can gauge the multiplicity of living beings which already existed when our earth was at that stage of development.

A momentous cosmic event here occurs. The sun withdraws, and simultaneously certain forces leave the earth altogether. These forces are composed of a part of that which was present on the earth hitherto in the form of life, chemical and light-ether. Thus these forces were withdrawn, as it were, from the earth as it had existed up to the present. Thereby a radical change took place in all the groups of terrestrial beings who had hitherto contained these forces within themselves. They underwent transformation. The first to be so transformed were what we called above the plant beings, who were deprived of the forces they had possessed by means of the light-ether, so that they could now only develop as living beings when acted upon from without by the light forces taken from them, and in this way plants came under the influence of sunlight.

Something of a similar nature

THE FIRST, OR POLAR, RACE

happened to the human bodies as well. Their light-ether had to co-operate henceforth with the light-ether of the sun, in order to be capable of life. But not only those beings from whom the light-ether had been directly withdrawn were affected; others were also influenced; for everything in the world works together. The animal forms, too, which did not themselves contain light-ether had once been irradiated by their fellow-beings on the earth, and developed under the influence of the light received from them; and they now came also indirectly under the influence of the sun from without. The human body, however, in particular, developed organs which are susceptible to the sunlight—the first rudiments of the human eye.

The result of the sun's separation is a further condensation of the matter of the earth. Solid matter began to develop from the liquid; in like manner the light-ether differentiates into a second kind of light-ether and an ether which enables bodies to develop warmth. The earth thus becomes a being which generates heat within itself. All its inhabitants were brought under the influence of heat. Again, in the astral world a similar process to the former one must occur: certain beings progressed at the expense of others. A certain number of beings, suited to work upon the gross solid matter, were separated off, and this was the origin of the firm skeleton of the earth, the mineral kingdom.

At first, the higher kingdoms of Nature did not all exercise their influence on this solid, mineral, bony mass, so that we find on the earth a mineral kingdom which is hard, and a vegetable kingdom in which the densest matter is water and air. For in this kingdom the gaseous body itself had been densified to a water-body by the events described; and, besides these, there were animals of the most multifarious forms, some with water and some with air-bodies. The human body itself had undergone a process of densification. Its firmest corporeality had solidified to the density of water. The heat-ether having arisen, this water-body of man's was pervaded by it, imparting to it a kind of matter which might, perhaps, be described as of the nature of gas. This condition of matter of the human body is described in works on Occult Science as that of "firemist." In this body of firemist man was incorporated.

X

THE SECOND, OR HYPER-BOREAN, RACE

In the last chapter the Akashic studies are carried to that point of time at which man's soul is incarnated in the subtle matter of the firemist. We must understand very clearly that man only assumed dense matter, which he now regards as his own, at a later date, and then only very gradually. If we wish to form an idea of his bodily appearance at the stage of his development just depicted, we can best do so by thinking of it as water-vapour, or as a cloud floating in the air; but this representation is, of course, one which merely approaches the reality superficially; for the fiery-cloud "man" is inwardly vitalised and organized. But in comparison to that which he becomes later on, we must picture him at this stage as psychically slumbering, as yet but dimly conscious. All that we can call intelligence, understanding and reason, are yet lacking in him. He moves about with a floating, rather than pacing, motion by means of four limb-like organs, forwards, backwards, sideways and in all directions. But as regards the soul of this being, something has already been said.

We must not think, however, that the movements, or other expressions of life evinced by these beings, were irrational or unregulated. On the contrary, they were perfectly regulated, and nothing happened without purpose and meaning, the only difference being that the guiding power, or understanding, was not within the beings themselves; rather were they controlled by an intelligence outside themselves. Higher beings, more fully developed than they, hovered round them, as it were, and guided them; for that is the all-important and fundamental quality of the firemist, that human beings at this stage of evolution could incarnate in it, while at the same time higher beings could also incorporate therein and could thus be in full intercommunication with man. Man had developed his inclinations, instincts and passions, up to a point at which they could clothe themselves in the firemist; but the other order of beings here mentioned could, by the power of their reason, create within this firemist, by means of their intelligent activity. For these latter possessed still higher faculties by means of which they could reach up to higher regions. From these regions their determinations and impulses emanated, but the actual effects of these determinations were apparent in the firemist. All that was done on the earth by man originated in the regulated intercourse of the human firemist body with that of those higher beings.

We can therefore say that man strove to climb upwards; in the firemist he was to evolve higher qualities—in a human sense—than he had possessed before. The other beings, however, strove downwards towards the material. Their course of evolution was to seek expression for their creative forces in ever denser and denser material forms; but in a wider sense this in no wise meant a degradation for them. We must come to a very clear understanding on this point: it requires higher power and capacity to control denser than rarer forms of matter. These higher beings, too, had in former periods of their evolution a power limited in extent as that of man at the present time. And they, like man to-day, once had dominion only over that which took place within them; they had no control over the outer coarse matter. They now strove to reach a condition in which they should magically direct external things, and were, therefore, at this period ahead of man in evolution. Man reached upwards, striving first to embody the mind in finer substances, so that it could afterwards direct its activity outwards. He had already assimilated reason and now became possessed of magic power in order to permeate with reason the surrounding world. Thus man advanced upwards through the stage of the firemist, while his companions pressed downwards through the same stage in order to increase their power.

The forces which above all others were most effective in the firemist were those known to man as his lower passions and impulses. Man, as well as the higher beings, makes use of these forces at the firemist period described; and these forces, working at that stage within the human form, have the effect of developing organs which enable man to think, and thus to develop his personality. In the higher beings, however, these forces worked at the stage with which we are now

THE HYPERBOREAN RACE

dealing, in such a manner that the beings mentioned could make use of them in order impersonally to bring about terrestrial conditions through their medium. By this means there arose on the earth, through these beings, forms which were themselves an image of the laws of reason. Thus, through the activity of the passional forces, there appeared in man the personal reasoning organs, and round about him, by means of the same forces, organizations replete with intelligence were formed.

Let us now think of this process as a little farther advanced, or rather, let us bring before us what we find registered in the Akashic Records, when we glance at a somewhat later period. The moon has separated from the earth; a great revolution has thereby been accomplished. A great part of the heat has escaped from the objects surrounding man, whereby these objects have passed into a coarser and denser order of matter. Man must live in this colder environment, and he can only do so by altering his own matter; and a change of form goes hand in hand with this densification of substance. For the condition of firemist on earth has itself given place to one which is entirely different. The result of this is that the higher beings spoken of, no longer have the firemist as a medium for their activity. Nor can they consequently any longer exercise an influence over the expression of man's soul-life, formerly their chief sphere of activity. But they have obtained power over the human form which they themselves had before created of the firemist.

THE HYPERBOREAN RACE

This change of activities goes hand in hand with a transformation of the human form. One half of the latter, with two motory organs, has been transformed into the lower half of the body, which has thus become mainly the vehicle of nutrition and generation. The other half is, as it were, directed upwards. Out of the two other organs of motion grow rudimentary hands. And such organs as had once also served for nutrition and generation are remodelled into organs of speech and thought. Man stands upright. That is the immediate consequence of the moon's exit. And together with the moon the terrestrial globe is deprived of all those forces which, in the period of the firemist, had enabled man to practise self-fructification and to bring forth beings like himself, without external influence. The whole lower half of his body—that which we often call his lower nature—is now subject to the formative influence, governed by reason, of those higher beings. That which these beings had themselves been able to regulate before in man, while the volume of forces, henceforth withdrawn into the moon, were still united with the earth, must now be organised by them with the co-operation of the two sexes. This explains why the moon has been regarded by Initiates as the symbol of generative forces, these forces clinging to it, as it were.

The higher beings, described above, being akin to the moon, are in a certain sense, moon-gods. Before the separation of the moon, they worked by its force in man;

afterwards their forces worked from outside to effect the propagation of man. We may also truly say that those exalted spiritual forces which were formerly acting upon man's still higher instincts through the medium of the firemist, have now descended to unfold their powers in the realm of reproduction. Lofty, divine forces are actually at work in regulating and organising this function.

In this we have the expression of an important teaching of Occult Science, which says that the high and sublime god-like forces are akin to the—apparently—lower forces of human nature. The word "apparently" must here be understood in its full significance; for it would be a complete misconception of occult truths to regard the force of generation in itself as something ignoble. It is only when man misuses this force and compels it to serve his passions and desires, that evil lurks in it; but not when he ennobles it by the thought that it contains divine, spiritual strength. Then will he place these forces at the service of the evolution of the earth, and will carry out the plans of those higher beings by means of his own generative forces. To raise this entire domain and place it under divine laws—not to destroy it—is what Occult Science teaches us. The latter can be the only result of superficially understood occult principles, distorted into mistaken asceticism.

We see that man had developed in the upper half of his body something over which the higher beings we spoke of had no influence; over

THE HYPERBOREAN RACE

this part other beings now obtain authority. They are those who had, indeed, at earlier stages of development advanced beyond humanity, but had not yet risen so high as the moon-gods. They could, so far, develop no power in the firemist; but now that a later condition has appeared in which, through the firemist, something in man's reasoning organs had attained development, something to which they themselves had approached earlier—now their time had come.

In the case of the moon-gods, the stage at which reason worked and organised outwardly had arrived earlier. In them this reason was present at the beginning of the firemist epoch. They could act outwardly on terrestrial objects, but the beings just described had not at an earlier period attained the development of an outwardly active reason, and therefore the firemist period found them unprepared. Now, however, reason is there. It is present in man, and they seize this human reason in order that they may work upon the things of earth through it. Just as formerly the moon-gods had worked upon the whole man, these work now on his lower half only, whereas the influence of the lower beings spoken of is at work upon his upper half.

Thus man is subject to a twofold guidance. In his lower nature he is subject to the power of the moon-gods, but in his evolved personality, he has come under the leadership of those beings called collectively by the name of their regent "Lucifer." For the Lucifer-beings complete their own evolution by making use of the awakened forces of man's reason. They could not attain this stage earlier. But they confer on man at the same time the disposition towards freedom, the tendency to distinguish "good" from "evil." Under the sole guidance of the moon-gods the human reasoning organ is indeed formed, but these gods would have allowed the organ to slumber; they would have had no interest in using it for themselves. They had their own powers of reason. The Lucifer-beings had an interest in developing human reason, in guiding it to the objects of earth for their own sake, and therefore they became for humanity the teachers of all that can be accomplished through man's reason. They could, however, be no more than instigators. For they could not develop reason in themselves, but, as we have seen, they could only do so in man. There arose thus a twofold stream of activity on earth. The one, arising from the direct influence of the moon-deities was regulated from the beginning by law and reason; for the moon-gods having already finished their time of apprenticeship, were now beyond the possibility of error. On the other hand, the Lucifer-gods, who had intercourse with man, had first of all to work their way to the light of such knowledge. Under their guidance man had to learn the laws of his nature; under the guidance of Lucifer he must himself become as "a god among Gods."

The question arises: if the Lucifer spirits had not progressed in their evolution to the point of intelligent creation in the firemist, where did they fall behind? Up to what stage in the earth's evolution were they able to co-operate with the moon-gods? The Akashic Records show us that they were able to take part in earthly creation up to the period at which the sun separated from the earth. We are shown that up to this time they performed what, it is true, was work of a somewhat inferior nature to that of the moon-gods, but nevertheless they belonged to the band of divine creators. After the separation of earth and sun, an activity —the work in the firemist—began on the former for which the moon-deities were prepared, but not the Lucifer-Spirits. For these, a period of inactivity and waiting then began.

Now, when the universal firemist had rolled away and the human beings began to work on the formation of their intellectual organs, the Lucifer-Spirits could again emerge from their period of rest. For the creation of reason is correlated with solar activity, and the dawn of intelligence in human nature is the rise of an inner sun. This is affirmed not merely figuratively, but in an absolutely real sense. These beings found thus an opportunity of resuming their activity within the human being, in conjunction with the sun, when the firemist epoch had passed away from earth. From this it is easy to see the origin of the name "Lucifer"—that is, "Lightbearer"—and why these beings are characterised in Occult Science as "sun-gods."

* * *

The readings from the Akashic Records describing the first beginnings of our earth and its inhabitants are to be found in "An Outline of Occult Science"—the most important of Dr. Steiner's works which has so far appeared—in the fifth chapter entitled "The Evolution of the World and Man." The reader will there find the present studies of the Akashic Records traced back to the origins of what we find in the world to-day.

INDEX

AIR, denser in Atlantis, 20 et seq.; denser in Lemuria, 90.

AIR-SHIPS, Atlantean, 19.

AMBITION, of Atlanteans, 33, 40.

ANCESTOR, Physical-, 175; with two principles, 180; Soul-, 174-5; -worship, of Atlanteans, 34.

ANIMAL kingdom, first, 203; -life in Lemuria, 111 et seq.; -life left behind by humanity, 164; unisexual, 161 et seq.; -like beings, 163; -men, 91.

ATLANTEAN airships, 19; communities, 34 et seq.; forefathers, 10; settlement, 10, 22. et seq.

ATLANTEAN sub-race, 1st. (Rmoahals), 28 et seq.; 2nd. (Tlavatli), 33 et seq.; 3rd. (Toltec), 36 et seq.; 4th. (Original Turanians), 41 et seq.; 5th. (Original Semite), 41 et seq.; nucleus of 5th. Root-Race, 44, 60, 70; transition into 5th. Root-Race, 57-78; 6th. (Akkadian), 44 et seq.; 7th. (Mongolian), 47 et seq.

ATLANTEANS, ambition of, 33, 40; ancestor-worship of, 34; memory of, 12 et seq., 48; mental capacity of, 11; physical strength

of, 22; power of, 40 et seq.; social instincts of, 23; thought-power of, 26.
ATLANTIS, aspect of man and nature in, 22-23; position of, 7; submerged, 8.

BEINGS, astral-human, 199; higher, 154, of second race, 215; plant-like, 207; semi-superhuman, 140, 156-160; spiritual, 154; superhuman, 133 et seq., 153, 156; of love, 139-141; of wisdom, 140-141.

COLOUR-PICTURES, 190-192.
COMMONWEALTH, Toltec, 36-39.
COMMUNITIES, growth of, 33; Toltec, 38 et seq.

DEATH, beginning of, 182.

EDUCATION, in Atlantis, 13 et seq., 37.; in Lemuria, 84 et seq.; of Toltecs, 38.
ETHER, Vital or life, 200-206; chemical, 200-206; heat, 210; light, 205-209.
ETHERIC HUMANITY, 199.
EYE, one, 192 et seq.
EYES, two, 193.

FALL, into Sin, 129.
FEELINGS, Development of, 146.
FIFTH ROOT-RACE, aim of education of, 76; and the development of thought-power,

INDEX

26, 66-67; transition from the Atlantean sub-race, 51-78.

FIRE, applied to human industry, 68 et seq.; natural and artificial, employed in Lemuria, 108 et seq.

FIREMIST, 212-226.

FIERY-CLOUD MAN, 214.

FIRST ROOT-RACE, 183, 167-194.

FORCE (see Life Force), reproductive, 121; soul-, fructified by mind, 124.

FORCES (see Natural Forces), division of soul-, 121 et seq.; god-like, akin to lower human, 223; of generation, not ignoble, 223 et seq.; passional, 218.

FORM, human, of Lemurians, 109-111; influenced by intellectual power, 110; single-sexed human, 123.

FREE WILL, the beginning of "good and evil," 159-160.

GENERATION, by cleavage, 167; by man of his own heat, 185, 210; influence of Spiritual Beings on, 155; regarded as sacred, 156; special organs of, 179; spontaneous, 146-147.

GENERATIVE FORCES, not ignoble, 223 et seq.

GERM, astral, 198; earth, 197; **plant, 196.**

GERMS, soul-, 138.

GODS, man a god among, 228; messengers of the, 54, 59-64, 72; moon-, 222-228;

sun-, 230; thou shalt have no other, etc., 64.

GOOD AND EVIL, began with free will, 159-160; originated by woman, 95; tendency to distinguish, 227.

HANDS, growth of, 221.
HEAT-ETHER, 210.
HEAT, Self-Generation of, 185, 210.
"HIGH SCHOOLS," of the powers of will, etc., 89.

IMAGINATION, and Lemurian Women, 85 et seq., 94 et seq.; female element of the soul, 119.
INITIATE, the greatest human will be publicly revealed, 76.
INITIATES, agreement of communications given out by, 6-7; and their schools, 15-16; human, 74-77; king-, 39; Lemurian, 93; of the 5th Atlantean sub-race, 72-73.
INITIATION, in Atlantean times, 39; origin of, 38.
"INITIATION AND ITS RESULTS," 3.
INNER LIFE, beginning of, 191.
LAW AND LEGISLATION, origin of, 47.

LEADER, Chief, of the 5th Atlantean sub-race, 60-64.
LEADERS, Divine(, 53 et seq., 62 et seq.; of

INDEX

pre-Lemurian humanity, 135-140; injunction of the Manu concerning the Higher, 62 et seq.

LEMURIAN CONTINENT, Position of, 79; era, 79-88; education of boys, 84-85; education of girls, 85 et seq.

LEMURIANS, buildings of the, 86 et seq.; dwellings of the, 86; instinct of the, 89; language of the, 82; mental conceptions of the, 82 et seq.

LIFE FORCE, loss of power over the, 43 et seq.; misuse of the, 40 et seq.; Mongolian belief in the, 43-49; used by the Atlanteans, 17 et seq.

LIFE PRINCIPLE (Prâna), 180.

LOVE, Force turned outwards, 133; Leaders of, 138 et seq.; of man before the division of sex, 134; of the superhuman beings, et seq.; sensual, 133-137; sexual, 155 et seq.

LUCIFER, 140, 226-230; beings, 227, 228-229; gods, 228; spirits, 228-230.

MALE AND FEMALE BODIES, development of, 118 et seq.; elements of the soul, 119.

MANU, a human, 76; and the 5th Atlantean sub-race, 60-77; injunction of the, concerning the divine leaders, 62 et seq.

MATTER, astral, earth composed of, 197-198.

MATTER, dense, requires high powers to control, 217; etheric, earth composed of, 198-199; solid, develops from liquid, 210; solidification of, 172, 179, 210, 220.

MEMORY, and speech, 29-30; formation of the germs of, 94; lack of, in the Lemurians, 27-30, 81; of the Atlanteans, 12 et seq., 48; of the Mongolians, 48; or recognition of deeds, 33-35.

MENTAL Capacity of the Atlanteans, 11; conceptions of the Lemurians, 82 et seq.

MORAL Conceptions originated in Lemurian Women, 95-96.

MESSENGERS of the Gods, 54, 59-64, 72.

METALS and stones softer in Lemuria, 110-111.

MIND CONCEPTIONS, development of, 158; the eternal part of man, 165; fructifies the inner soul-force, 124 et seq.; the influence of, on the Male and Female Souls, 125-126.

MINDLESS, the, 162.

MOON, the Symbol of the Generative Forces, 222; the withdrawal of the, 188, 219 et seq.

MOON-GODS, 222-223, 225-228.

NATURAL FORCES, interpreted by woman, 96; Lemurian mastery of, 88; used by the Atlanteans, 29.

NATURE, and the Lemurian Women, 94;

and the picture-consciousness, 153-154; loss of command over the forces of, 43; man's relation to, in Atlantis, 22-23, 31 et seq.; the kingdom of, in the First Race, 195 et seq.

ORGANS, four limb-like, 214; mental, 161; motory, 145, 221; of feeling, 146; of hearing, 145, 178, 184; of generation formed, 179; of sight, 192-193; of speech and thought, 221; of touch, 184; reasoning, 218, 227; soul-, 193.
"OUTLINE OF OCCULT SCIENCE," referred to, 231.

PERSONAL EXPERIENCE, growth and recognition of, 38-39.
PHYSICAL STRENGTH of the Atlanteans, 22.
PICTURE-CONSCIOUSNESS, 147 et seq., 174.
POSEIDONIS, the island of, 7-8.
PRIESTESSES, Description of Lemurian, 106.

REASON, human, and the Lucifer beings, 227 et seq.; human, and the moon-gods, 225-226; organs of, appeared, 218.
REBIRTH, of the soul-life, 183.
ROOT-RACES, sevenfold, 27; the first two, 183 et seq.; transition of the 3rd and 4th, 27 et seq.; transition of the 4th and 5th, 51 et seq.

SECOND ROOT-RACE, 183, 213-230.
SELFISHNESS as the outcome of sex-division, 133 et seq.
SENSATION, of first two root-races, 184; the beginnings of, 181.
SENSE, of feeling, 146, 152; of hearing, 146, 152; of hearing, 146, 148, 152, 184; of sight, 189, 190; of touch, 146, 184.
SEPARATION, of sexes, 121 et seq., 146, 193; of sun and moon, 189 et seq.
SEXUAL, love, 155 et seq.; desire, 155-156.
SOCIAL groups, formation of, 35 et seq.; instincts of the Atlanteans, 23.
SOUL-Ancestors, 175; -life drawn into sphere of physical matter, 186; -organs (Nervous System), 193; -tree, 176; male and female, 118-119, 124-124, 134.
SPEECH, development of, 29 et seq.; nature-, of Lemurian women, 104-105 et seq.; regarded as sacred, 32.
STONES and metals softer in Lemuria, 110-111.
"STORY OF ATLANTIS," 8.
SUN, the withdrawal of the, 189, 207.
SUN-GODS, 230.

TEMPLES of Mysteries, 55.
THIRD Root-Race, 79-97.
THOUHT-POWER, Aryan development of, 26; of the 5th Atlantean sub-race, 41 et seq.,

INDEX

51 et seq.; of the 6th Atlantean sub-race, 44 et seq.; of the 7th Atlantean sub-race, 47-49.

TOLTEC Commonwealth, 36-39; communities, 38.

WATER, more fluid in Atlantis, 21; more fluid in Lemuria, 90.

"WAY OF INITATION," the, referred to, 3.

WILL, Lemurian Control of the, 84, 88 et seq.; male element of the soul, 119; "the religion of the —," 92.

WOMAN in Lemuria, 85-86, 94 et seq., 99-115.

WORDS of Power, 31 et seq.

WORSHIP, Atlantean places of, 87 et seq.

LaVergne, TN USA
17 February 2011
216974LV00001B/71/A